Canada on Fire

CANADA ON FIRE

Jennifer Crump

DUNDURN PRESS
TORONTO

Project Editor: Michael Carroll
Editor: Cheryl Hawley
Design: Courtney Horner
Printer: Marquis

Library and Archives Canada Cataloguing in Publication

Crump, Jennifer
        Canada on fire : the War of 1812 / by Jennifer Crump.

Includes bibliographical references and index.
Issued also in an electronic format.
ISBN 978-1-55488-753-8

        1. Canada--History--War of 1812--Juvenile literature.
I. Title.

FC442.C77 2010   j971.03'4   C2010-902436-2

1   2   3   4   5   15   14   13   12   11

We acknowledge the support of the **Canada Council for the Arts** and the **Ontario Arts Council** for our publishing program. We also acknowledge the financial support of the **Government of Canada** through the **Canada Book Fund** and **The Association for the Export of Canadian Books**, and the **Government of Ontario** through the **Ontario Book Publishers Tax Credit**, and the **Ontario Media Development Corporation**.

Care has been taken to trace the ownership of copyright material used in this book. The author and the publisher welcome any information enabling them to rectify any references or credits in subsequent editions.

J. Kirk Howard, President

Printed and bound in Canada.
Printed on recycled paper.
www.dundurn.com

Dundurn Press
3 Church Street, Suite 500
Toronto, Ontario, Canada
M5E 1M2

Gazelle Book Services Limited
White Cross Mills
High Town, Lancaster, England
LA1 4XS

Dundurn Press
2250 Military Road
Tonawanda, NY
U.S.A. 14150

Danielle, Kathleen, Alexandria, Emily, Laura, and Alex …
as always, the most supportive family anyone could ever have.
Thank you.

TABLE OF CONTENTS

CHRONOLOGY

1811

November 1811   The Battle of Tippecanoe (Prophetstown)

1812

July 2   The Capture of the *Cuyahoga Packet*

July 17   The British Capture Fort Mackinac

July 4   The Lachine Riot

August 15   The Fort Dearborn Massacre

August 16   The Fall of Fort Detroit

August 20–September 8   The Dearborn-Prevost Armistice

October 13   The Battle of Queenston Heights

1812–1815   Shipbuilding on Lake Ontario

1813

January 18–22   The Battle of Frenchtown: The River Raisin Massacre

February   March Overland Trek to Kingston

April 27   The Battle of York

May   The Siege of Fort Meigs

May 29   Invasion of Sackets Harbor

September 10   Battle of Lake Erie

October 5   The Battle of Moraviantown (The Battle of the Thames)

October 26   The Battle of Châteauguay

November 10   The Battle of Chrysler's Farm

1814

March 30	The Battle of Lacolle Mills
July	The Road to Lundy's Lane: Niagara Campaign of 1814
July 25	Battle of Lundy's Lane: Niagara Campaign 1814
August–September	The British in Chesapeake Bay: The Washington Campaign
September 11	The Battle of Plattsburgh Bay
December 24	The Treaty of Ghent
January 8	The Battle of New Orleans

CHAPTER ONE:
BROCK THE BOLD

For most of the 10 years that Major-General Isaac Brock had been stationed in Canada, he had wanted nothing more than to leave. The career soldier yearned to be where the real action was — on the battlefields of Europe, fighting Napoleon. But instead he was stuck in Fort George, an old wooden fort outside the town of Newark, Upper Canada (present-day Niagara-on-the-Lake, Ontario), waiting for a war that might never happen. He had sent several letters to the Prince Regent — the head of the British armed forces — requesting permission to return to England, but to no avail. His boredom and frustration with life on the Niagara frontier is reflected in a letter he wrote to his brother in 1811, "You who have passed all of your days in the bustle of London, can scarcely conceive the uninteresting and insipid life I am doomed to lead in this retirement."[1]

Blonde, blue-eyed, and well over six-feet-tall, Brock was a dashing figure in his scarlet uniform. At 42, he was the commander-in-chief of all the troops in Upper Canada, but Brock had no illusions about the realities of his new position. The troops he commanded were ill-equipped and frequently insubordinate. Within months of his arrival he was forced to chase a group of deserters across the border into the U.S. in order to bring them back and court martial them. But most of the men under his immediate command respected Brock. He had seen battle, he was courageous. They saw him as a man of great destiny.

But would he find his destiny in the remote colonies? Brock very much doubted it. In the early 19th century, Canada, then known as "the Canadas," was a loose confederacy of villages scattered along the eastern half of the continent in two provinces, Upper Canada and Lower Canada (present-day Ontario and Quebec). Most of the colonials were farmers, and many were recent immigrants from the United States — Loyalists who had fled to Canada following the American War of Independence. The fluid border drawn after that war was still defended by a series of isolated wooden forts, most of which were in a state of frightening disrepair. The British soldiers who manned these forts buffered their isolation with rum and dreams of past victories.

When a letter arrived from the Prince Regent in early 1812, finally granting Brock permission to return to England, he should have been ecstatic. His opportunity had arrived. Fame and glory in the fight against Napoleon could be his. But by that time things had become a whole lot more exciting in the colonies. Every sign pointed to war with the Americans and Brock, as the acting political administrator of Upper Canada, felt duty bound to stay. His next letter to England requested leave to remain in Canada.

The colonials had whispered of war with the Americans for most of the decade, but recent rumours seemed to hold more substance. Some members of the American Congress were openly calling for war. Indeed, many of them believed that a war with Canada would barely be a war at all. Thomas Jefferson, the former American president, publicly declared that the acquisition of Canada would be, "a mere matter of marching."[2]

And so it might have been, for the odds seemed insurmountable. America's population was seven million; it had a trained army of more than 35,000[3] and an ample supply of arms. By contrast, Canada's population was barely half a million; it had only 5,000 British soldiers, a possible 4,000 militia, and very few arms.[4]

All able-bodied Canadian men could have been called up to serve on the militia, but Brock thought it prudent to arm only 1,500.[5] He knew that few had any deep attachment to Britain, and fewer still could be counted on to commit to a war they saw as a fight between the British and Americans. At that time, Brock had little respect for the Canadian militia. He believed that they were ill-trained and ill-equipped, and that they would desert at the first opportunity. However, within the next few months the general's opinion about Canadian fighting men would change.

On June 19, 1812, while at a formal dinner with his American counterparts at Fort George, Brock was informed that President Madison had officially declared war on Canada. The officers, who had frequently socialized until then, politely finished the meal before returning to their respective headquarters to plot strategy. The whispers of war became a deafening shout as word spread. No one doubted the outcome. Canadian politicians, civilians, and the Native peoples believed an American victory was inevitable. Brock desperately needed the Native peoples as allies, but they were reluctant to back the losing side. They had far too much to lose. No one, it seemed, had counted on Isaac Brock. "Most of the people have lost confidence," he wrote to one of his brothers. "I, however, speak loud and look big."[6]

A Matter of Timing

So many things might have been different if communications had been a little more reliable during the War of 1812. In fact, it is possible that the war would not have taken place at all. Two days before Congress declared war, the British agreed to repeal all of the laws the U.S. objected to. Unfortunately, it was several weeks before news of the repeal finally reached North America and by that time the war was well underway. President Madison would later say that he would have stayed the declaration of war if he had been aware of the concessions that Britain had made.

Throughout the war, channels of communication were precarious at best. Roads were virtually nonexistent and relaying information was a ponderous, dangerous undertaking. Communications were frequently intercepted by the enemy. To add to the confusion, sympathizers on both sides were not above distributing misleading or faulty communication in order to misdirect enemy troops.

Poor communication did have some positive effects. For months, Brock was able to do as he pleased, preparing for the war in the absence of direct orders from his superiors. But in a final irony, the last and bloodiest battle of the war could have been avoided if communication lines had been improved. The Battle of New Orleans was fought 15 days after the Treaty of Ghent was signed.

A natural leader with a reputation for boldness and quick thinking, Brock's ability to bluff was legendary. In his youth, he had once been challenged to a duel. As the one challenged, he was given the choice of weapons. To everyone's surprise he chose pistols, even though his opponent had a reputation as a crack shot. As the details of the duel were discussed, Brock declared that the duel would not be fought at the usual 30 paces. Instead, he and his opponent would fire at each other over a handkerchief. His opponent balked, refused the duel, and was subsequently forced to quit the British Army in disgrace.

This kind of quick thinking helped Brock even the odds with the Americans before the first volley had even been fired. As soon as he heard that war had been declared, Brock passed the news on to his commander at Fort Amherstburg (now called Fort Malden, in present-day Amherstburg, Ontario), more than 300 kilometres away at the northwest end of Lake Erie. Shortly after Brock's courier arrived at the quiet fort on the banks of the Detroit River, the American schooner *Cuyahoga Packet* blithely sailed past on its way to Fort Detroit, Michigan. A young French Canadian lieutenant at the fort, Frederic Rolette, ordered a British captain and six sailors into a longboat. The men calmly approached the *Cuyahoga Packet*, boarded her, and told the captain and crew they were prisoners of war. The Americans were stunned — they'd had no idea that war had even been declared.

The capture of the *Cuyahoga Packet* had provided Brock with some critical information. The boat had been carrying correspondence from William Hull, an American general who was slogging his way through the forests of western Michigan en route to Fort Detroit. Hull, it turned out, was also oblivious of his country's declaration of war.

The correspondence found on the *Cuyahoga Packet* confirmed what Brock had already suspected. Once Hull reached Fort Detroit, he would launch an attack on the village of Sandwich, near Fort Amherstburg. The correspondence also revealed that Hull had greatly overestimated his enemy's strength, and that he was terrified at the prospect of fighting the Native warriors who were aligned with the British. Further, Hull's own army was small and largely demoralized. Few among the American militia had any enthusiasm for fighting a war on foreign soil.

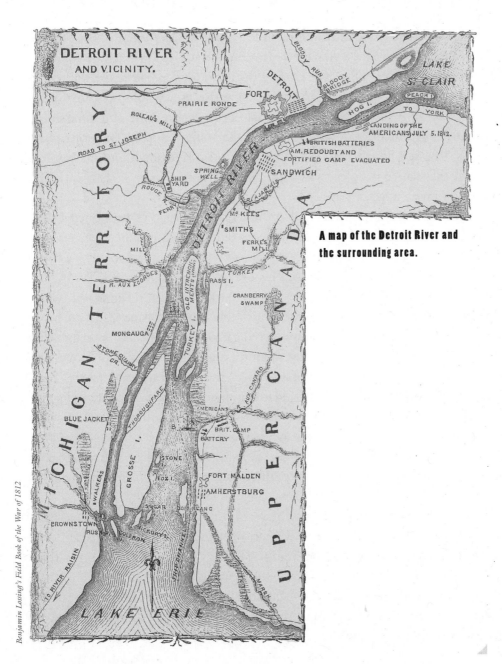

A map of the Detroit River and the surrounding area.

Benjamin Lossing's Field Book of the War of 1812

Brock estimated it would take Hull at least four weeks to reach Fort Detroit, and he planned to pay him a visit there. But first he arranged to deliver a blow to the Americans on another frontier. During the tedious years before the war, Brock had been quietly placing his men in strategic areas so they would be ready for the Americans' opening move. Now that war had been declared, he sent a missive to Robert Dickson, one of his few allies among the Native peoples. Dickson, a Scot known as "the red-haired man," had married a Sioux woman and his loyalties were with the Native peoples, who had accepted him as one of their own. He considered himself a Sioux warrior.

Dickson and his 250 warriors had already joined a group of pensioned British soldiers at St. Joseph Island in the northern arm of Lake Huron. When they received word from Brock on July 17, the warriors and old soldiers, accompanied by a handful of fur traders, immediately followed his orders. Under cover of darkness, they silently paddled across Lake Huron to Michilimackinac Island. The island, which had been reluctantly abandoned by the British following the American War of Independence, had been crucial to the western fur trade — and would be again. After quietly waking the villagers and taking them to safety, the old soldiers, along with Dickson and his men, confronted Porter Hanks, the American commander. Terrified at the sight of the Native warriors, Hanks immediately surrendered the fort.

For Brock, it was an important moral victory, albeit a bloodless one. His men had won the first battle. The victory also sent a clear message to the Native peoples: the British were willing to fight and able to win. The distribution of spoils from the capture sent another message: there were reward to be had if one sided with the British.

While his men had been achieving glory at Michilimackinac, Brock had been stuck in York (present-day Toronto, Ontario), begging the politicians for arms and the authority to call up the local militia. He was desperate to be in the thick of things and was eager to be on his way to engage General Hull.

Hull had already occupied Sandwich, and Brock expected him to attack the vulnerable Fort Amherstburg at any moment. But while Brock shored up the weak defences of Amherstburg with every spare soldier and weapon he could find, his superior, Sir George Prevost, the governor general of Canada, was attempting to negotiate a peace. Brock was frustrated. He was afraid the war would be over before he had a chance to see action. And he firmly believed that any peace negotiated with the Americans would not last. Finally, in early August, Brock convinced the legislature to allow him to call up the militia. Five-hundred men answered the call. However, with few supplies or arms, Brock could only afford to take half of them.

During the voyage along the length of Lake Erie, Brock and his army were caught in a storm. When the storm died the wind died with it, and the men were forced to row their way across. Brock's own boat hit a rock. In full dress, he climbed overboard to help dislodge it. When the group was underway once again, he opened his personal stock of spirits and handed every man on board a glass. That, and similar acts of generosity, endeared Brock to his men.

Once they had landed, Brock allowed the exhausted soldiers to sleep. But the driven leader pressed on toward Fort Amherstburg. It was long past midnight when he reached his quarters at the fort. Before he had a chance to fall into bed, there was a loud knock at his door. Outside was Lieutenant-Colonel John Macdonell, Brock's aide-de-camp. Standing next to Macdonell was a tall, lithe warrior who was promptly introduced as the Great Tecumseh, a Shawnee war chief.

Brock and Tecumseh eyed each other. Tecumseh saw a tall, broad-shouldered soldier. A soldier of intelligence and action. A leader not unlike himself. "Here is a man!"[7] he would later exclaim to his fellow chiefs.

Brock, too, was impressed. He wrote to his brother, "A more sagacious and gallant Warrior does not, I believe, exist. He was the admiration of every one who conversed with him."[8] The two men shook hands and Brock called a hasty war conference. While Brock's junior officers pleaded caution, Tecumseh pushed for immediate action. Brock, sensing a like mind, agreed with him. But action was all but impossible while Prevost and government officials in both Canada and Great Britain were dead set on a defensive strategy.

Despite orders from his superiors to retaliate only if the Americans attacked first, Brock immediately attempted to provoke a fight with General Hull. On August 15, he ordered an artillery barrage of Fort Detroit. Then he audaciously demanded that the Americans surrender. Safe within the walls of the fort with a large contingent of soldiers, Hull, not surprisingly, refused.

Later that night, after the gunshots had faded into silence, Brock sent Tecumseh and 500 of his Shawnee warriors across the Detroit River. Once across, they silently surrounded the fort and stayed hidden in the dense forest.

With 500 Native warriors, 700 local militia, and barely 300 regular soldiers, Brock knew his men were hopelessly outnumbered. He used two strategies that he became famous for. He ordered the British soldiers to give the militia their spare uniforms. There were not enough uniforms to go around, so they shared them — a bright red jacket here, a pair of white breeches there. On the morning of August 16, after leading this ragtag army across the river, Brock organized the men into columns and ordered them to march at twice the usual distance from one another. To the Americans watching from the fort, Brock's troops seemed twice as numerous as they really were. Brock rode at the head of the line, his great height and red and gold uniform making him an easy target. When an aide suggested that Brock would be safer somewhere within the column, he refused. He would not, he said, ask his men to go where he was not willing to lead.

Just as the British came within range of the American guns, Brock veered off and led his men into the safety of a nearby ravine. Remembering Hull's fear of Native warriors, Brock had ordered Tecumseh to parade his troops across a field in full view of the fort immediately after the army and militia had taken refuge in the ravine. The warriors crossed the field, disappeared into the forest, and doubled back to the place where they had begun their march. Then they marched again — and again. General Hull was convinced he was facing 1,500 warriors.

The terrified Hull, who had his daughter and grandson inside the fort, asked for a three-day truce. Brock gave him three hours, then frightened the hapless general even more by warning him that the Native warriors would "be beyond control the moment the contest commences."[9] Hull immediately surrendered the fort.

Brock and Tecumseh rode into the fort side by side. Brock was resplendent in his uniform, and wore a beaded sash — a gift from Tecumseh — tied around his waist. Tecumseh, in his far simpler fringed buckskin, looked equally impressive.

Brock had, it is said, gifted Tecumseh with his own military sash. But Tecumseh, with a customary lack of conceit, had given it to Chief Walk in Water, whom he considered of higher rank than himself.

Brock had won another decisive victory. With the capture of Fort Detroit, most of the Michigan Territory was in British hands. Many of the Native peoples, who had so far stayed neutral in the conflict, declared for the British. The militia and the Upper Canada legislature were also buoyed by Brock's success.

Canadians were exhilarated. They began to think there was a chance that the American invasion could be resisted after all. Brock had captured an entire army — more than double the size of his own — and taken control of a territory as large as Upper Canada. It was a tremendous feat. But of more immediate importance to Brock was the cache of weapons, supplies, and coin that the victory had brought the British forces. He knew that the war had just begun. He also knew that if the Americans had any tactical sense at all, they would attack on several fronts. Reasoning that the enemy's next target would be the Niagara frontier, Brock handed over command of the Detroit area to one of his subordinates and hurried back across Lake Erie to Fort Niagara.

Before he reached the fort, Brock heard news that threatened everything he had achieved. Governor General George Prevost had negotiated a one-month truce with the Americans. The truce had gone into effect on August 8, a week before Brock had taken Fort Detroit, though no word had reached either the British or Americans there. Brock, eager to act on the momentum he had built, was bitterly disappointed. The Native peoples were outraged. They wondered if they had backed the wrong side.

In Niagara, Brock was hailed as a hero. He was a little stunned by the adulation he received but slowly began to "attach to it more importance than I was at first inclined."[10] He used his new heroic status to convince the legislature to call up more militia, but he was unable to convince Prevost to build on these victories by launching an immediate attack on the American fortifications across the Niagara River. In America, even while their General Hull was being court-martialled for cowardice, Brock had achieved a near mythic status as a man of

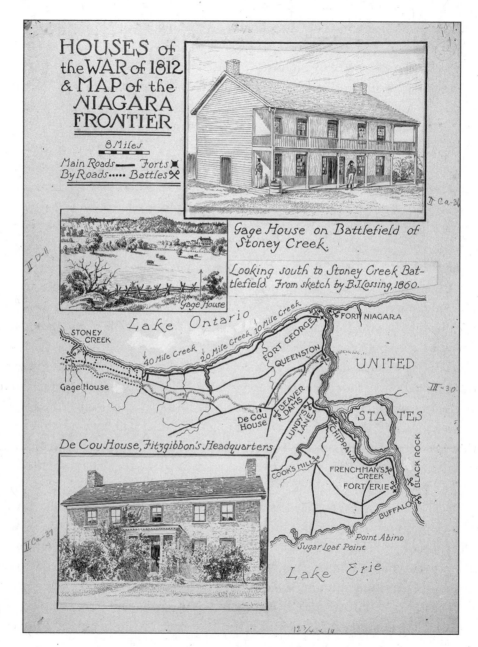

HOUSES of
the WAR of 1812
& MAP of the
NIAGARA
FRONTIER

8 Miles

Main Roads ——— Forts
By Roads ····· Battles

Gage House on Battlefield of
Stoney Creek.

Looking south to Stoney Creek Battlefield. From sketch by B.J.Lossing, 1860.

De Cou House, Fitzgibbon's Headquarters

**Houses of the War of
1812 and the Map of the
Niagara Frontier.**

unparalleled courage and honour. An incident that demonstrated this unfailing sense of honour occurred earlier in the war. A Canadian commander had landed his vessel along the Lake Erie shore and raided several American farms. When he heard about it, Brock was furious. He ordered the ship back under a flag of truce. The property that had not been destroyed was returned to the owners, along with funds to cover the rest.

During the truce, Brock spread the 1,000 regular troops and 600-strong militia along the 37-kilometre Niagara frontier, all the way from Fort George in the north to Fort Erie in the south. Few thought this thin red line would hold. Brock concentrated most of troops at Fort Erie and Chippawa, where everyone expected the Americans to attack first. He held back 600 militia and Native warriors, who would be immediately deployed as reinforcements once the attack came, as Brock and nearly everyone — except the colonial government — were sure it would.

Brock was under no illusions. He believed that the Americans were using the truce to reinforce their positions. And he was right. He arrived in Fort George on September 6, two days before the truce was scheduled to end. By that time, the Americans had managed to muster more than 8,000 troops, half of them regulars. These troops were now gathered along the American side of the Niagara River facing down Brock's very thin red line.

Realizing he was facing a significantly larger force, Brock wrote to Prevost requesting reinforcements. Prevost refused. He still believed that no invasion would take place on either frontier as long as the British did nothing to antagonize the Americans. He instructed Brock to maintain a defensive posture only, and even asked him to consider abandoning Detroit and the Michigan area and move those troops east to the Niagara frontier. This was unacceptable to Brock. He knew the current support of the Canadian people, the militia, and the Native peoples was tied directly to his victory at Detroit. Abandoning that victory could very well lose him that support.

Brock was first and foremost a soldier. He obeyed commands. Even though he believed he could sweep the entire Niagara frontier if given the opportunity, he did not attack. But he did not abandon the Michigan territories either.

The frustrated Brock knew the Americans would have to attack soon to keep their restless troops under control. A number of American regulars had already defected to the British, carrying with them tales of impatience and insurrection among the American regular troops and militia. The American militia was no happier with the war than the Canadians were. Most were reluctant to fight their former neighbours, and militia pay and rations offered them little incentive. Brock set up a system of beacon signals along the Niagara frontier to warn of the coming attack. Then he waited.

On the night of October 11, the few soldiers stationed at the village of Queenston, 10 kilometres south of Fort George, listened avidly to the sounds of a botched invasion attempt from the Americans. Armed and anxious to start the fight, the Americans had boarded boats to take them across the Niagara River to the village. To their dismay, they discovered that all the oars had been stored aboard another boat. Unfortunately for them, that boat, and the sailor in charge of it, had disappeared. No one was sure whether that was by chance or design.

The Americans and Canadians sat out the night behind their own borders while a massive storm whipped up the already rough waters of the river. The wait took its toll on the soldiers of both sides. In the morning, Brock received word that his own soldiers in Queenston had threatened to shoot their superiors if action did not begin soon. Brock immediately dispatched a trusted officer, Captain Thomas Evans, to investigate the mutiny and bring back some of the worst offenders. Evans did not have to ask what would happen to the mutineers he brought back. Years before, Brock had arrested a group of Fort George soldiers who had mutinied against their commander. The mutineers were taken out and shot in front of the entire company. While Brock could be humane, even jovial, he was also ruthless when necessary.

Brock also commanded Evans to negotiate an exchange of British soldiers and sailors with American Major-General Stephen Van Rensselaer. When Evans returned that evening, he reported that he had released all the mutinying soldiers in Queenston, believing the group could earn their parole in the coming fight. The officer also told Brock that he had been denied entry into Van Rensselaer's camp. This incident, along with other news he had heard, made Evans conclude that an attack on Queenston was imminent.

Brock's staff officers dismissed Evans's report. After all, rumours of impending attack had been incessant since the end of the truce more than a month before. Brock, although also skeptical, called up the Queenston militia and ordered them to join the two companies of the 49th Regiment, the Grenadiers Company, and the Light Company, who were already there. The Grenadiers quartered in a stone guardhouse in the village while the Light Company camped atop the escarpment above the village. With the militia and regulars, a mere 300 men guarded Queenston.

At 4:00 a.m. on October 13, 1812, Brock was awakened in his quarters in Fort George by the booming canons of a furious artillery assault on Queenston. Had the battle begun? Was Queenston the true target? Or was this a feint to draw attention away from the real attack on Fort George? Anxious to see what was happening, Brock leapt onto his horse and galloped toward the battle, pausing only to order an artillery unit and a party of Mohawk warriors to follow him; his aide-de-camp, Macdonell, raced after his general, but he could not catch him. Two other aides, who had not even had time to dress, lagged hopelessly behind.

As Brock struggled through the mud on the ride to Queenston, he encountered a young York militiaman who had been dispatched to tell him the enemy had launched their attack. In the heat of battle, no one had thought of using Brock's carefully planned signal fires. Angry at the oversight, but excited at the prospect of battle, Brock urged his horse forward in a furious gallop. The York Volunteers, a militia unit, were already moving toward the besieged village. Brock waved them on as he thundered past.

Queenston was a tidy little village with no more than 20 houses scattered within its boundaries. On that fateful morning, it had already survived Mother Nature's fury in the form of a wicked fall thunderstorm. Now the town was buffeted by yet another tempest. This one was courtesy of the Americans — and far more deadly.

As Brock rode into the village the Grenadiers cheered him. He saw they were holding the enemy — barely — and galloped past. He headed directly for the escarpment above the village, where the men of the Light Company were protecting the Heights. As soon he reached the top, he ordered these men to go back down the hill to help the Grenadiers wrest control of the village.

Brock was left with only an eight-man gunner team. The men aimed the 18-pound cannon at the America shore, pounding the river and shoreline with artillery fire. Brock intently surveyed the scene below him. Cannons on both sides roared incessantly. Shells burst in the air above the river and the village. The bright, brief flare of muskets lit up the murky dawn. Across the water, he saw hundreds of the enemy waiting their turn to board the boats and cross to Queenston. Sailors valiantly rowed empty boats back to the American side to pick up more men, shells splashing into the water all around them.

Then Brock heard an unexpected and spine-chilling sound from behind him — a battle cry. He spun around to see an American force cresting the Heights. The gunners barely had time to spike their gun, rendering it unusable, before they scattered down the hillside. Brock quickly followed, leading his horse by the reins because he had not even had time to remount.

When he arrived in the village, Brock took refuge in one of the abandoned houses. By that time, Macdonell had finally reached the village and found his general. Brock instructed him to send for reinforcements and then weighed his options. The situation was desperate. He could try to retake the Heights without the help of the reinforcements, which would be extremely hazardous, or he could wait. Reinforcements would take too long to get there. The Americans would use that time to ferry over more men and consolidate their positions. Without control of the Heights, Brock believed Upper Canada would be lost. Once the Americans gained a foothold in Queenston, they would have cut his thin red line along the Niagara frontier in two.

Brock was not a man to hesitate. With typical bravado, he mounted his horse and galloped through the village. He rallied some 200 soldiers, and an equal number of weary, dazed local militia — men he was now proud to lead. "Follow me boys," he yelled as he thundered toward the base of the ridge, where he took cover behind a wall. "Take a breath," he shouted a moment later, "you'll need it in a few moments."[11]

The soldiers cheered.

Before the cheers had died away, Brock charged up the hill. His soldiers struggled to keep up on the slippery footing of wet leaves. No one was close enough to their general to urge him to slow down and take cover among them. Once again, Brock was an easy target. This time, he took a bullet in his wrist. The wound slowed him down, but he pressed on, waving his sword.

On the Heights above them, the Americans had fanned out. Hidden among the trees and foliage, they continued firing their muskets at the British and Canadian soldiers as they crested the hill. Many bullets found their mark. One found Brock. "Are you much hurt, Sir?" one of the militiamen asked anxiously.[12] Brock did not reply. With his hand clutching his chest, he sank to the ground. The bullet had pierced his heart — he died instantly.

The stunned soldiers crowded around their fallen leader, barely able to grasp that Brock, a man who seemed invincible, was dead. Mud splattered his face, and blood soaked his jacket and the beaded sash. He no longer looked like the elegant general they knew; but he was not diminished in their eyes. As they stood rooted to the ground, a cannonball sliced one of the men in two and the corpse fell on Brock's body. This prompted the horrified soldiers into action. They retreated, carrying their general's body back down the hill.

Even in death, Brock was victorious. His demise spurred on both the British and Canadian soldiers, who were determined to avenge their fallen hero. Macdonell gallantly led two more unsuccessful attempts to retake the Heights. He was wounded in the second attack and died later that night.

The reinforcements — soldiers and a group of very determined Mohawks — finally arrived and joined Brock's troops in the fight. Together, they pushed the Americans out of the village. On the ridge, the British, led by General Roger Sheaffe, advanced on the American line with bayonets fixed. The line collapsed and the Americans fled to the edge of the escarpment. Some fell to their deaths;

The Death of Brock at Queenston Heights.

others managed to make it to the beach, where they waited in vain for boats that never came. Many others hid in the crevices of the escarpment, waiting for their leader to surrender.

U.S. Lieutenant-Colonel Winfield Scott tried. He had sent two men on separate missions to surrender. Both had been killed by incensed Native warriors who had seen the Americans kill their men. Finally, the American commander went himself. He made it through, barely, and his surrender was accepted.

Brock's forces had won the day, recapturing both the Heights and the village. But this was no bloodless victory. The American toll was 300 killed or wounded and 925 taken prisoner. The British and Canadians suffered only 15 deaths and

CANADA ON FIRE

70 wounded. But the victory was bittersweet to soldiers and citizens alike because it had cost them their well-loved hero.

One young militiaman wrote to his brother, "Were it not for the death of General Brock and Macdonell, our victory would have been glorious … but in losing our man … is an irreparable loss."[13]

A friend of Brock's from Quebec, one of the many ladies he had charmed, wrote, "The conquest of half the United States would not repay us for his loss. By the faces of the people here you would judge that we have lost everything, so general is the regret everyone feels for this brave man, the victory is swallowed up in it."[14]

On the morning of October 16, the caskets of Brock and Macdonell were carried from Government House in Newark to Fort George. Throngs of people came out to witness the solemn procession. Inside the fort, the pallbearers carried the two caskets between rows of more than 5,000 troops, militia, and Native warriors so they could pay their final respects.

A 21-gun salute broke the silence as Brock and Macdonell were lowered into a single grave. Moments later, the salute was echoed as soldiers on the American side also paid their respects to the fallen general.

Brock's confidence in Canada's ability to repel the Americans had been shared by very few people. With his death, Canadians had a hero to mourn and a common cause to rally behind. If they could not follow the general into battle, they would follow his vision.

For Tecumseh and the Native warriors, the loss of Brock was a terrible blow. They had lost the one British soldier they admired and trusted, the man who had promised them a homeland. But their lot had been cast. There would be no withdrawal. They would remain with the British to see the war to its end.

Far away in England, church bells rang in Sir Isaac Brock's memory. For his capture of Fort Detroit, the Prince Regent had made him a Knight of the Order of Bath. But as Brock was charging the Heights at Queenston, news of this honour was still slowly making its way across the Atlantic and Brock never learned of it.

In Brock's hometown on the small island of Guernsey, Channel Islands, his family crest was changed to include the figure of a Native warrior, reflecting his family's pride in the unique relationship Brock had forged with Tecumseh and the Native peoples of Canada.

In one short year, Brock had managed to inspire a nation. He was the stuff legends are made of. Following his death, the myth and legend of Brock became larger than the man himself. The soldier, who had once wanted nothing more than to leave Canada, was destined to spend all of eternity there as a symbol of loyalty and courage. Brock left a legacy of confidence to the people of Canada; confidence in their leaders and, more importantly, confidence in themselves. They were going to need both in the coming months.

CHAPTER TWO:
THE VOYAGEURS

The gate to Fort Michilimackinac slowly swung open to admit a small, solemn group of chiefs and warriors. The chiefs were invited guests but the sentries at the gate were still apprehensive. They been raised on stories of Native barbarity and they could not understand why their own commanders had requested this meeting. They watched nervously as the Natives rode past, the rider's expressions betraying nothing of their thoughts or intentions.

A few moments later, the group took their seats around a rough wooden table in the commanding officer's house and accepted the gifts offered by the Americans. In return, they were willing to listen to what the Americans had to say, but they would promise nothing else. The American governor general rose to persuade them to ally themselves with the American fort and to avoid contact with the British and the North West Company at Fort St. Joseph on the other side of Lake Huron. The response was quick and unanimous. The First Nations had already pledged their allegiance to the British, they would not switch sides. "Ignore the post at St. Joseph," the governor general thundered, "because we will seize it before the end of the summer." The Natives remained unmoved and made their way out of the fort as quietly as they had arrived. They wasted little time in sending a messenger to Fort St. Joseph. With his angry words, the governor general had ensured that the North West Company received advance notice of the war that was about to be declared. The Nor'Westers wasted no time preparing.

A war with the States could prove disastrous for the North West Company. Formed by a group of hardy Scottish fur traders and based in Montreal, their acknowledged intention was to dominate the fur trade in the West. But they were facing a number of significant challenges. They were already locked in a trade battle with their traditional rival, the Hudson's Bay Company. While the Hudson's Bay Company shipped their furs through Hudson Bay, the North West Company had established an easily accessible route to the West through the St. Lawrence and French Rivers. They had also taken a different approach to trade. Rather than having the Natives come to them with furs, they went to the Natives, establishing trading posts deep in the interior. The tactic was proving to be a great success and it attracted the attention of an American entrepreneur by the name of Jacob Astor, who was lobbying hard for his own monopoly on trade in the American West. Astor had already sent explorers out to stake territory and was in the process of building a fort he called Astoria, on the Columbia River. Encouraged by the American government, settlers were slowly drifting west and creating friction with the fur traders and their Native allies as they competed for land. The American government was anxious to secure the West, which gave them another, perhaps more important, reason to go to war. The North West Company was already feeling the pressure of competition and a war that threatened their supply route could destroy them. This combination of threats and a mutual interest in protecting supply routes would make them one of Canada's greatest allies.

With traders and loyal Natives spread across the West, the North West Company had an established communication and intelligence network that was the envy of both standing armies. They also preferred to use express post rather than regular mail, therefore they were informed of Madison's declaration of war long before the British knew and even before the American soldiers at Fort Michilimackinac received the news. In fact, a North West Company agent working in New York City had overheard news of Madison's declaration of war and had immediately forwarded that intelligence on to company headquarters via express. The company quickly shared the information with the government and army. The highest ranking British diplomat in the United States failed to forward any news, standing firm in his belief that the Americans would withdraw the declaration if they remained unprovoked. The North West Company, like Brock, was equally sure that war was inevitable and swung into action.

From his offices in Montreal, the head of the company, William McGillvray, ordered his voyageurs to map out another supply route they could use in the event that Lake Erie was blockaded. This alternate route would take them from York through to Lake Simcoe and Georgian Bay, and was in place long before the first American attack occurred. As the new route was being explored, a group of local fur traders, under the leadership of Lewis Crawford, approached the commander at Fort St. Joseph to offer their services. Robert Dickson, another trader with deep ties to the local Native community and a fierce loyalty to Britain, also brought several hundred Sioux, Menominee, and Winnebago warriors to the aid of the small group of soldiers manning the fort. Over 200 Chippewa and Ottawa warriors arrived shortly after with yet another trader, John Askin Jr.

Despite these unexpected reinforcements, few thought that Fort St. Joseph would be able to withstand an attack. It had been built in an exposed position that made it exceedingly difficult to defend. The highest ranking officer at the fort, Captain Charles Roberts, commanded only a handful of men, the majority of whom were long past their prime or had been wounded and were now considered unfit for active service. Most, Roberts would later write, "Were so debilitated and worn down by constant drunkenness, that neither fear of punishment, the love of fame or the honour of their Country could animate them to any extraordinary exertions."[1] The voyageurs who joined them were an equally motley crew and yet Roberts and Dickson agreed they had little choice. They would have to launch a pre-emptive strike if they wanted to save Fort St. Joseph. The North West Company men were in full agreement. Fort Michilimackinac had once belonged to the British, who had given it away as part of the treaty that ended the Revolutionary War. The North West Company had protested then and now they were more than willing to make up for what they considered to be a British tactical error.

In July, a North West Company ship arrived at Fort St. Joseph after taking a mere eight days to travel all the way from Montreal.[2] On board was a company man by the name of William MacKay. MacKay was one of those interesting hybrids that the only North West Company seems to produce, a man as comfortable in the deep bush as he was in the ballrooms and boardrooms of Montreal. The Scottish immigrant had joined the North West Company when he was 18 and spent years exploring North America's most isolated regions, establishing close ties with the Native tribes who lived there and taking the time to learn their languages and cultures. He married his first wife, a Native woman, according to the custom of the country[3] and quickly became one of the company's top traders. By the time he retired in 1809, MacKay was a partner in the company, a member of the elite Beaver Club,[4] and an established member of Montreal's most exclusive society. His "country" wife chose to remain behind and quickly remarried to another fur trader. MacKay also remarried, this time to the daughter of a prominent local judge.[5]

With both the North West Company and the colony under threat, MacKay once again offered his services. His Montreal superiors provided him with a ship and tasked MacKay with delivering the news to the fort that war had been declared and it was critical that he get to Captain Roberts as quickly as possible and without being detected by the Americans. The ship barely laid anchor before MacKay climbed overboard into a waiting bateau that took him to Fort St. Joseph. Across the lake, the American fort was still in the dark. The letter from the government informing them they were at war had been sent through the regular channels and didn't arrive until it is far too late. On July 15, Roberts and Dickson drew up a quick plan of attack. Eager to retake the fort that had been lost to them after the Revolutionary War, the North West Company offered a ship to transport troops and opened up its storehouses to the soldiers. They also provided the gifts that finalized and secured alliances with the warriors who had gathered to help.

Across Lake Huron, the commander of Fort Michilimackinac, Lieutenant Porter Hanks, had been taking note of the numbers of Native warriors who were paddling up the Lake toward the British fort. He had also noticed that the encampment of Natives normally set up just outside his walls was virtually empty. He saw no reason for immediate alarm — war had not been declared yet so there could be no reason for the British and Canadians to attack. Still, Hanks was a man of caution so he called in a member of the local militia to conduct a reconnaissance mission. The militiaman set off in his canoe at sunset on July 16 and was barely 16 kilometres away from the fort when he encountered a terrifying sight.

CANADA ON FIRE

MACKINACK, FROM ROUND ISLAND.[4]

A View of Mackinac from Round Island.

At first he could only make out a handful of war canoes, but as he drew closer to them he threw up his hands in surrender. A ship surrounded by a flotilla of 10 bateaux and over 70 canoes quickly surrounded him. Questioned on board, the militiaman mistakenly revealed an interesting bit of information: the Americans within the fort still had no idea that war had been declared.

The Canadians quickly paroled the American militiaman and sent him back to Mackinac Island with strict parole conditions. He was not to reveal the impending invasion to the fort. Instead, he was instructed to head for the village where he was to encourage all villagers to take refuge on the western part of the island until the battle was over. In the meantime, the Canadian invasion force pulled their canoes and bateaux onto the beach and slowly made their way to a large point of high land, known locally as the Turtle's Back, that overlooked the fort. From the ship, the voyageurs dragged several canons up onto the Turtle's Back. They immediately set up the canons to take aim on the "most defenceless part of the garrison."[6] The warriors had slipped into the forest surrounding the fort and were making no effort to conceal themselves. In fact, they made as much noise as possible. By 9:00 the next morning, Porter Hanks was certain that a force of 1,000 men had his fort surrounded and was equally sure that his force of less than 60 men could not possibly hold them off. A contingent of men from the village soon arrived, flying a flag of truce and carrying a request from the British: surrender or we will be forced to destroy the fort. It seemed hopeless. By noon, Porter had the colours struck and surrendered the fort. Not a single shot had been fired.

Fort Michilimackinac was back in the hands of the British. The North West Company was lauded by friend and foe alike. Even its rival, the Hudson's Bay Company, acknowledged their significant contribution to the war effort. The route to the West through the narrows between Huron and Superior was secure and would remain so until the end of the war. Word of the bloodless victory quickly reached both Sir Isaac Brock and General William Hull, causing the latter to pull back to Fort Detroit. This small victory turned what had appeared to be an early American advantage into a Canadian and British opportunity. Weeks later, the Canadians, British, and their Native allies would take Fort Detroit as well, ensuring that the western front was secure.

The North West Company was still completely committed to the war effort. McGillvray appealed for volunteers from among the hundreds of voyageurs who worked for the company with the hopes of formalizing their military contribution. One of the first to step up to offer his services was William MacKay. By October 1st, hundreds had answered McGillvray's call and the British embodied the first Corps of Canadian Voyageurs with McGillvray as its commandant. The British even offered the new unit a set of bright red uniforms, but the voyageurs balked at wearing them. They argued that the British uniform was impractical for the northern bush. Instead, much to the chagrin of the disciplined British troops, the voyageurs insisted on wearing their traditional attire: moccasins, loose leggings, a thick woollen overcoat made of blankets, and a distinctive red toque on their heads. The British issued each man a sword, pike, and pistol but many were either discarded or sold off. The voyageurs were far more comfortable with their tomahawks, knives, and axes.

Portrait of William McGillivray.

The main purpose of the unit was to protect the supply lines to the West, but they would also see action in several key battles. Still, many members of the British high command believed the voyageurs were more trouble than they were worth. The British Army was built on strict discipline and the voyageurs prided themselves on a definite lack of discipline. The British officers sent to train them experienced no end of frustration. Pranks and public intoxication were an issue and the men would often appear on the parade grounds, unshaven, unkempt, and decidedly unwilling to parade. They suffered from an excess of humour that compounded their commanders' frustration. Whenever they encountered an officer, no matter what his rank or marital status, they would take off their hat, perform a deep bow, and greet the officer with a cheerful, "Hello General!" followed up with an equally saucy, "How's the wife?" When summoned to duty, they would generally report with a pipe in their mouth and their ration of pork and bread stuck to their bayonets.[7] For those, and numerous other infractions, the voyageurs were occasionally, and briefly, imprisoned. But even imprisoned, they could not be held. If the guard happened to be a fellow voyageur, it was more than likely that the prisoner would be let out to spend the evening at home with his wife and his supper, with a promise to return in the morning.

Lack of discipline aside, the voyageurs were very well-suited to the type of war that was being fought in the northwestern woods in 1812. There were few large-scale battles but many minor skirmishes and small raids. The unit saw its first entanglement a few weeks after it was formed when a small group of voyageurs, including one of McGillvray's sons, was dispatched to convince the Mohawks of St. Regis to join the British cause. At their improvised picket just outside the village, along the New York and Lower Canada (Quebec) border, they were surprised by a force of several hundred American soldiers. Six voyageurs, including the young McGillvray, were killed. Another 50 voyageurs were captured and taken prisoner. In November, MacKay and a group of his fellow voyageurs were manning a blockhouse in Lacolle Mills when the Americans attacked. With a typical instinct for innovation and self-preservation, the voyageurs slipped away under cover of nightfall, leaving the empty blockhouse to the Americans.

The American "victory" quickly turned to tragedy when another American force arrived at the blockhouse later that night and the two forces engaged each other in a fierce battle, each believing they were facing the enemy. It was already morning when they realized that the Canadians were nowhere to be found and that they had been fighting their own men. In January 1813, another contingent of voyageurs helped deliver a devastating defeat to the Americans at the Battle of River Raisin.

While they contributed men and expertise to the war effort, the North West Company had not forgotten the other challenges to Canada and, more importantly perhaps, to its own business interests. In 1812, there were no firm boundaries set up between the Canadian colonies and United States in the newly opened West. John Astor had planned to set up a series of forts in the far West to secure his access to furs and cement American hegemony in the area. But the war interfered with his plan and in 1813 only one fort — Astoria — had been established, high on the Columbia River. The fort was just over a year old when its inhabitants noticed a small flotilla of canoes slowly making its way up the last few kilometres of the river. The canoe in front, one of the broad freighter canoes favoured by the voyageurs, flew a Union Jack high above it. The small group drew their canoes, each loaded to the gunnels with furs, up on the shores opposite the fort. The Nor'westers had arrived.

One of the leaders of the group — John George McTavish — led a delegation to request a meeting with the fort's manager, Duncan McDougall. McTavish boldly informed McDougall that since Fort Astoria was an American colony they were the enemy. Demonstrating the ingenuity the Nor'westers were legendary for, McTavish further informed McDougall that his own canoe was merely part of the advance party. Any day now, the ship *Isaac Todd* would arrive, accompanied by the armed frigate *Phoebe*. Better that McDougall surrender the fort now, McTavish advised, before the battle was engaged. McDougall could probably have defended the fort, even against an armed frigate, but he was a manager, a fur trader with little appetite for war. Within hours, the Stars and Stripes had been hauled down and the Union Jack was flying in its place. McDougall was handed $53,000 for the fort to forward to his boss, John Astor, and the men inside were granted back wages owed to them and transportation home if they wished it. Neither the *Isaac Todd* nor the *Phoebe* ever appeared, but weeks later another ship appeared on the Columbia River. The Nor'Westers were nervous. What if the ship was American? Would their ruse hold up? They had a few hours of nervous waiting before it was finally identified as the British sloop *Raccoon*. It had come to capture Fort Astoria and the men who manned it were sorely disappointed to find that the prize had already been taken — by a few fur traders in a half-dozen canoes!

In March 1813, Britain disbanded the Corps of Canadian Voyageurs with effusive words of praise for their contribution to the war effort. But less than one month later the unit was reformed under the control of the provincial commissariat. Again they were given the task of protecting the supply lines. In the spring of 1814, William MacKay was promoted to the rank of brevet major and given command of the Michigan Fencibles, a unit whose soldiers were largely drawn from voyageurs living near Lake Michigan. The commander of the post reported that the decision to put MacKay in control was a wise one as he "was popular with the Fencibles and all Canadians."[8] Shortly after receiving his promotion, MacKay and the Fencibles received their first assignment. The Americans had taken Prairie du Chien on the Mississippi River and were busy building a new fort named Shelby at the rear of the village. MacKay was dispatched to take the village and the fort.

The Americans were still working on the fort when MacKay and his fellow voyageurs arrived in July 1814. Five Winnebago had lost their lives in the American jail at the fort, reportedly for trying to escape, and their brethren now joined MacKay in his effort to destroy the fort. Shortly after arriving, MacKay dispatched several of his men under a flag of truce to deliver an offer to the fort's commander, Lieutenant Joseph Perkins. "Surrender unconditionally or be prepared to fight to the last man," he wrote. If they chose the latter, MacKay requested that the women and children of the fort be released to find a safe haven before the battle began. Confident that his new fort could withstand the British onslaught, particularly with the aid of the well-armed gunboat *Governor Clark*, which was moored on the river just outside the village, Perkins refused the surrender.

Voyageurs at Dawn.

Realizing the danger posed by the canons on the *Governor Clark*, MacKay ordered his guns to focus on the gunboat. What MacKay did not know was that the *Governor Clark* was carrying most of the fort's ordnance and ammunition. After several direct hits, the gunboat began to take on water. The sailors scurried about the deck attempting to cut the cables holding it moored and exposed. As the gunboat began to drift downstream, the voyageurs watched in fascination as the Americans in the fort fired a shot across the boats bow in an effort to force it to stop its retreat. The effort did not work and soon the gunboat was downstream, out of range of MacKay's guns. He ordered the guns to focus on the fort and for two days a fierce gun battle raged.

Inside the fort, Perkins was running out of ammunition and hospital supplies. There was no more water. The well had caved in during an attempt to dig it deeper in order to locate more water. Finally, and with much reluctance, Perkins was forced to offer to surrender. MacKay agreed to accept the American surrender but asked them to delay exiting the fort for another day in order to ensure their safety

THE VOYAGEURS

with the still infuriated Winnebago. The next day, the Americans slowly filed out of the fort. MacKay had placed a contingent of Dakota between the Americans and the Winnebago. Reportedly, that did not stop one American from losing all the fingers from one hand when he attempted to shake the hand of a Winnebago. MacKay promptly paroled most of the American soldiers and sent them with an escort toward the relative safety of St. Louis. On hearing of his victory, the British renamed Fort Shelby to Fort William in MacKay's honour. Finally, MacKay lead his troops back to Lake Huron just as his fellow voyageurs were successfully fending off an American attempt to retake Fort Michimilimackinac.

For the remainder of the war, MacKay resumed his old job of ensuring that supply routes were kept open and that supplies made their way safely to the northwestern forts. In this capacity, he was expected to provide escorts to canoes and supply ships, as the Americans were actively targeting the North West Company ships and supply routes. On August 4, American forces burned the abandoned Fort St. Joseph to the ground and looted the company supply stores in Sault Ste. Marie. Then they seized the company ship the *Mink* and captured the *Perseverance*. Only the *Nancy*, a supply ship, managed to escape. Her crew had been warned of the impending American attack by a voyageur who had paddled alongside. The *Nancy* hid near Georgian Bay, but eventually the Americans found her and destroyed her too. The Americans finally left, leaving two ships — the *Scorpion* and *Tigress* — to maintain a blockade. Not about to accept defeat, once night fell the voyageurs and their Native allies slipped out of the fort and paddled up to the American ships. After a brief scuffle, they easily seized both and ended the blockade.

Once the war was officially over, MacKay was offered the position of deputy superintendent and agent of the Indian Department. When the terms of the treaty became clear to everyone, it fell to a disappointed MacKay to inform the voyageurs and Natives that the British had returned all of the forts they had taken to the Americans. Even Fort Michimilimackinac was restored to the Americans.

Despite the fact that they viewed the war as just one of a series of challenges they needed to overcome, the men of the North West Company made a tremendous contribution to the Canadian cause in the war against the States.

CHAPTER THREE:
JOHN NORTON AND
THE GHOST WARRIORS

While Brock charged forward in his last battle, another old warrior was silently leading his tiny troop back along the road to Queenston Heights. Partway along the road, the Mohawk war chief known as both Teyoninhokarawen and John Norton, and 50 of his Mohawk warriors slipped into the deep woods and began their own climb up the Heights. They had not chosen an easy route, but a precarious one that would bring them into direct contact with the American invaders. As Isaac Brock lay dying on the other side of the Heights, Norton rallied his troops, leading them in a furious and continuous assault on the Americans. War whoops rent the air, sending chills down the spines of the American militia. Some of the more terrified men threw themselves off the cliffs rather than face the Mohawks. The rest of the assault force remained pinned on the Heights while the British and Canadians waited for reinforcements to arrive before continuing Brock's assault. The Mohawks did not waver, despite the odds that were so clearly stacked against them. They, and their war chief John Norton, were determined to see the Canadians carry the day. Things had not always been that way.

The Mohawks, like the rest of the Iroquois Confederacy, were initially ambivalent about their support for either side. This was not helped by the mixed messages they were receiving from the Indian Department, which, up until war was declared, was still encouraging the Iroquois to maintain the peace with the Americans in order to avoid sparking an Anglo-American conflict. The Confederacy was in a unique position, with villages scattered along both sides of the border. A secret meeting between members of the Confederacy on each side was held in order to encourage all of the tribes to maintain their neutrality with other delegates arguing in support of the British or the Americans. When war was declared, another delegation slipped over the border into Canada to press for neutrality. The appeal of a neutral position was enhanced when General Hull launched his invasion and guaranteed the safety of the Iroquois and their lands if they did not interfere. A call from Brock to send warriors to his aid at Fort George was met with the response that the Iroquois were too busy tending their crops to assist.

The Iroquois settled onto the fence and tried to maintain a precarious balance there. Since it seemed likely that the Americans, who commanded a much larger army, would win the war, they could not afford to break the appearance of neutrality. At the same time, they could not afford to appear treasonous should the British prevail. Their response to the invasion was to send a small party of warriors to the mouth of the Grand to "watch" for the arrival of American troops. Through other channels, Brock learned that the Iroquois had had face-to-face meetings with General Hull, but the Iroquois would only admit that Hull had captured a single Oneida warrior and sent him back to the Iroquois with a message of neutrality. Brock saw a definite threat to the British position and warned his superiors that the Iroquois would throw their support behind the American cause.

In York, Reverend John Strachan, then the rector at St. James Cathedral, was a little more charitable. He realized that it was not that the Iroquois preferred the enemy but that "they considered our case desperate and they thought by joining the Americans they could save their lands."[1]

The refusal of the Iroquois to join the British had other ramifications. Militiamen from the surrounding area refused Brock's call, worried that the Iroquois would turn on their wives and children while they were away fighting the Americans. For their part, the Americans did not need the Iroquois to join them, all they needed was an assurance that the Iroquois would not join the British. The British, on the other hand, desperately needed the Iroquois. For the time being it looked like the American sympathizers would hold sway, but what no one had counted on was the determination of John Norton.

John Norton's Cherokee father had been taken to Scotland as a boy, eventually joined the British military, and married a Scotswoman. Norton was born in Scotland in 1770. He received a good education, as his later writings would prove,

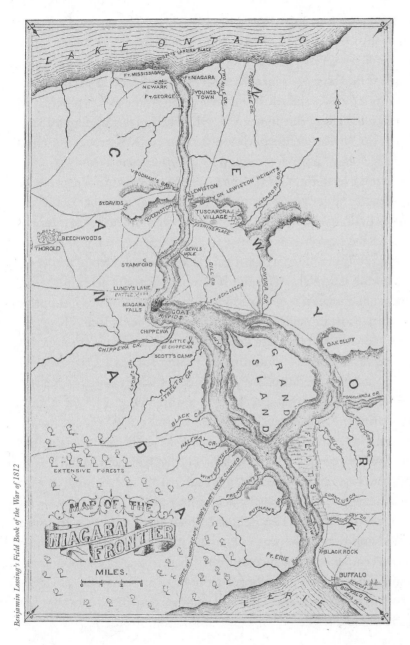

Benjamin Lossing's Field Book of the War of 1812

Map of the Niagara Frontier.

and was rumoured to speak four European and no less than 12 Native languages. Following his father into the military, he was sent to Ireland at age 14 and then served in Quebec. Military service proved not to be the experience he imagined and when his regiment moved to Niagara, Norton deserted. A dedicated traveller with an overwhelming case of wanderlust, he served for a time as a teacher in an Iroquois village before travelling throughout North America as a trader and later as an interpreter for the British. The conditions of the Natives he encountered depressed him and made him more determined to improve their lives.

Eventually he settled near the Grand River, where he became a protege of John Brant. He learned the language of the Mohawks and was eventually adopted into the tribe. Brant sent him to England to represent Mohawk interests there and to persuade the British government to allow them to sell a portion of their land, bypassing the Indian Department that at the time controlled, and often profited from, Native land sales. Though his mission was unsuccessful, Norton did make the acquaintance of several prominent Quakers. Through them he redeveloped his loyalty to Britain and his commitment to the church. He translated the Bible into Mohawk and brought copies home to distribute amongst his adopted peoples. He resumed his wandering, searching for his Cherokee relatives and developing contacts amongst the various tribes across North America. His travels reaffirmed his belief that the key to improving the lot of Native Americans was solidarity.

Norton possessed many skills and he had to employ all of them to navigate the turbulent waters of Six Nations politics. He was personally dedicated to the British cause and sure that the best chance the Iroquois had was to ally themselves with Britain. When the war began, Norton had once again returned to Mohawks. As a war chief he sat in on the councils that debated which side, if any, the Iroquois Confederacy should support, and he was unhappy with their decision to remain neutral. If Norton was convinced that success for the Native cause lay in solidarity, he was equally convinced that it lay in supporting the British. The events at Tippecanoe and the massacre of a group of pacifist in Delaware convinced him that the Americans wished to subjugate the Natives, not deal fairly with them.

Norton was not only fighting against competing interests with the Iroquois. His growing prestige had also attracted the interest and enmity of William Claus, the deputy superintendent general of the Indian Department. Norton, with good reason, viewed the Indian Department as inept and corrupt. He trusted the British military leaders and preferred to deal with them, effectively bypassing the Indian Department. Although Norton was able to accomplish things more quickly and fairly, his actions also served to increase the resentment of Claus and others who were determined to maintain control of their own profits. Claus began a determined effort to lobby some of the Native leaders and to plant seeds of doubt about just how well they could trust John Norton.

Norton was infuriated by the decision of the joint council to stay out of the war. In defiance of the decision of the council, Norton took a band of 60 warriors to aid the British in the bloodless capture of Fort Mackinac. The appearance of Norton's warriors terrified the Americans and contributed to Porter Hanks's decision to give up the fort so easily. Thirty of the warriors turned back before they reached Mackinac, perhaps having second thoughts about ignoring the decisions of their community. Once Mackinac was conquered, Norton marched the remnants of his small band west toward Fort Detroit. Along the way they were joined by Ojibwas and Ottawas. Soon, Fort Detroit was in British hands and the American General Hull had been forced into an embarrassing retreat.

Perhaps disappointed in the lack of support from his adopted tribe, Norton asked to remain in the West. But Brock had other plans. He needed Norton to renew his efforts to convince the Iroquois to throw their lots in with the British, which would convince the local militia that it was safe to leave their homes. Expecting an imminent attack in Niagara, Brock needed all of the help he could get. A skeptical Norton agreed but he could make no promises. Norton quickly discovered that things had changed since he and his warriors left for Mackinac. First, the expected easy American victory had turned into an embarrassing rout and Norton's arrival at the head of collection of warriors from a variety of tribes, all of whom appeared to support the British cause, convinced the Mohawks that they too should consider supporting the British. The loot the warriors returned home with ensured this support.

Norton was a hardened warrior who considered loot to be part of a soldier's portion. Stories of American soldiers and officers being stripped of all of their money and possessions and even the clothes off their backs, by warriors under Norton's command, soon filtered out of the West. Norton also arranged for the British to supply their Native allies with payments and gifts for their assistance so that the warriors would be able to support their families while they were away fighting for the British. By the time Brock reached Fort George on September 6, 1812, almost 500 Mohawks warriors had joined the war effort. Their reluctance to join a fight they could not possibly benefit from seemed like treason to Brock. He never entirely trusted their commitment to the cause.

Unlike Tecumseh, Norton's position as leader was never completely secure. He had to deal with the conflicting and occasionally fickle loyalties of the Iroquois. The well-placed enemies he had made in the Indian Department continually undermined him within the military hierarchy, and with his own people. Yet Norton was still able to convince Governor General Prevost to declare him grand chief of the Mohawks with sole responsibility for the distribution of presents and payment to the Iroquois. His prestige greatly enhanced, Norton was able to convince numerous young warriors to follow him. Though their numbers varied widely and were never great, Norton's warriors participated in nearly every major battle and skirmish on the Niagara front and were invaluable to the war effort. Norton himself was highly prized. Major Drummond remarked that, "This man is of the coolest and most undaunted courage and has led the Indians with the greatest gallantry and much effect on many occasions against the enemy...."[2]

Following his heroic efforts at Queenston Heights, Norton was promoted to the rank of captain, but neither he nor his Mohawks were given much time to rest. Less than one month later, the Americans were anxious to establish another foothold in Canada and to take revenge for their losses at Queenston Heights. American General Van Rensselaer, who was held responsible for the

John Norton, Teyoninhokarawen, Chief Mohawk.

JOHN NORTON AND THE GHOST WARRIORS

colossal American defeat at Queenston Heights, had been replaced by General Alexander Smyth. One of Smyth's first acts was to announce his plans to invade Canada within two weeks. He boasted long and loud enough that the British and John Norton were very well-prepared. On a moonless night at the end of November, the Americans quietly pulled up their bateaux on the Canadian side of the border. They grinned to see a lone Canadian sentry guarding the bridge over Frenchman's Creek, the only route for British reinforcements from Fort George and Chippewa. But the lone sentry was not truly alone. Waiting in the cover of the dense woods were militia, regulars, and John Norton's Mohawks. As the Americans approached the bridge, thrilled by the prospect of what looked like an easy victory, they failed to see the other soldiers and warriors slipping in amongst the trees. The Americans marched single file along the dark road and as they neared the bridge shots rang out. Over and over. The Americans fired wildly into the dense woods at targets they could not see and then they took cover in the woods. But the dark night made it hard to tell friend from foe and man after man on both sides fell to enemy and friendly fire. Over 200 soldiers died in the brief skirmish that followed, before a general retreat was called and the Americans scurried back to their boats.

Victory was short-lived for the Canadians and a flood of bad news for the British soon put their alliance with the Iroquois at risk. First York fell, quickly followed by Fort George. Many of Norton's warriors left the army to return to their territory on the Grand River. They hid their families and goods in the forest, fearing that they might be the next target for the American invaders. It was a clear opportunity for Norton's enemies and soon Claus was attempting to undermine Norton. He was too proud, too willing to risk Native lives, and perhaps too closely aligned with the British. Were the Mohawks his first concern? Or were they merely a means to an end? When the British decided on a counterattack they requested that 30 or 40 Mohawk join the attack. The Iroquois refused. Their first priority was protecting their families, not fighting a war that was starting to seem like a lost cause. Only Norton and a handful of warriors who continued to support him answered the British call to arms.

Norton and his warriors continually harassed the enemy with brief raids and lightning attacks that kept the Americans on the edge. They were the ghost warriors who slipped in and out of the woods, hitting the enemy hard only to disappear again if the battle turned. Their major strength lay not in their numbers, which were relatively small, but in the terror they struck in the hearts of the Americans. Scalping was still a common practice and they were more likely to kill than take prisoners. Having fought in nearly every battle on the Niagara frontier in 1812, John Norton and the Mohawks were also busy throughout 1813. They fought in the first major battle of that year at Stoney Creek, and when that battle was won they pursued the retreating Americans, taking prisoners and securing an enviable amount of loot from the supplies and weaponry that were left behind. After Stoney Creek, the Mohawks harassed the Americans up and down the Niagara River from a series of temporary encampments. In one such incident, a small group of Natives encountered and attacked a group of American soldiers on a reconnaissance mission from Fort Erie. They killed one soldier, wounded another, and then chased the remaining soldiers right into the middle of their camp, wreaking terror and confusion among the Americans.

Norton and his warriors' role was primarily providing support for the British and Canadian forces, but in the Battle of Beaver Dams they would provide much more than that. Two-hundred-fifty Native warriors, supported by 80 British regulars, were sent out to meet an American force along the narrow trail leading to Beaver Dams. An American scouting party caught sight of red uniforms in the distance but failed to detect the hundreds of Native warriors waiting in the woods. As the main column of the invasion force neared their hiding place the warriors stepped out onto the path and opened fire. The American cavalry unit was the first to charge the warrior line. The warriors were exposed on the road but they used a technique that had become their signature tactic. They attacked in waves, with the first wave retreating to reload before advancing to fire again. They also used the smoke from the musket fire to their advantage by changing their position after each volley. The Americans would try to fire on them only to realize they were not where they had been a few seconds before. The cavalry quickly wheeled around and attempted to retreat, ripping right through their own line of infantry.

The bulk of the Native force took over the attack from the safety of the woods, but the Americans had rallied and pursued them. Taking heavy casualties, the Natives withdrew, pulling the Americans deeper in the woods before reforming and resuming the fight. Eventually they were able to force both the American cavalry and soldiers into a hollow where the Americans surrendered. The Natives took prisoners and plunder from the captured Americans. The British would pay them $5 per head for some of the captured soldiers, while the Mohawks would keep others as slaves. One Mohawk chief took a young American soldier. The chief had recently lost his own son in battle. When the American pleaded with the British to save him, the chief responded that if the soldier behaved the chief might consider adopting him. All the British who watched could offer was advice: do as you're told and do not try to escape for a year or two, or they'll kill you.

In July 1813, John Norton angered the entire Indian Department by allowing a delegation of Six Nations from New York to attend a meeting with the Canadians members of the Six Nations. The British generals were worried that the meeting would only serve to undermine the already fragile commitment of the Canadian Six Nations to the war effort. But the meeting ended with a simple promise by the delegates, who primarily consisted of a single tribe — the Tuscaroras — to each keep to their own side of the border. Iroquois would not fight Iroquois.

Also in July, Norton remarried to a young Delaware woman named Catherine, providing Claus and the rest of the Indian Department with yet another opportunity to cause problems for him. Catherine was, they said, a common woman of questionable morals. To the Natives they pointed out that Norton was spending most of his time touring the countryside in a carriage with his new wife. But those proved to be only minor distractions for Norton compared to the news that filtered out of New York State at the end of the month. In New York the American Six Nations announced their support for the American cause and their declaration of war on the British. It looked as though the peace among the confederacy, and Norton's goal of solidarity, would not survive the war.

As the summer neared its end, an American regiment decided to dislodge a small group of British regulars who had set up a picket near Ball's Farm in the Niagara Region. The British called for backup and a contingent of Native warriors and Canadian militia, including a group lead by Norton, hurried to their aid. They scattered into the woods to lay ambushes for the approaching Americans. Norton's small group of warriors was discovered by an American scout, who they quickly disposed of. Following close behind the scout was a party of warriors who Norton stood up to greet before quickly realizing his mistake. The warriors were Iroquois but they were Seneca Iroquois fighting with the Americans. A fierce battle began and Norton was soon forced to retreat. Another party of warriors allied with the Canadians arrived and hurried to join the battle. They did not realize that Norton had retreated. The American warriors welcomed the group with whoops and muskets raised in the air, calling out to the Canadian warriors to join them. Fooled into believing they were among friends, the Canadians hurried forward. When they were a few yards apart, the American warriors levelled their muskets at the Canadian warriors, fired, and then rushed with their tomahawks. What ensued was a vicious battle that ended with five Canadian warriors dead, three wounded, and many taken prisoner.

Norton and many of his men believed that the Tuscarora had betrayed them. They vowed revenge. Their opportunity came in December 1813. In a daring nighttime attack, the British, assisted by Norton and his warriors, captured the American Fort of Niagara. Exhilarated by the easy win, the British and Norton's warriors celebrate with a night of drinking. One of the warriors mentioned that there was a Tuscacora village nearby — where they could easily take their revenge. Fuelled by alcohol and their thirst for vengeance, the soldiers and warriors looted the sleeping village and then razed it to the ground. This rash act prompted many previously neutral Iroquois to join the American forces and lead to a terrible confrontation, one that set brother against brother.

In July 1814, both sides were anxious to deal the blow that would end the war once and for all. The Niagara region had suffered more than most, particularly the tiny village of Chippewa. The Americans crossed the Niagara with a dual force —

one of which would attack Fort Erie while the other pursued the British force that was believed to be camped along the Chippewa River. Caught between the two armies once more, the Chippewa villagers fled to relative safety behind the British lines. Hearing of the American invasion, British Major-General Phineas Riall hurried forward to meet the Americans. With the American force divided, he believed the odds were in his favour. This was reinforced when Norton returned from a reconnaissance to report that the Americans numbered barely 2,000. Riall's 1,800 men stood an excellent chance. What Riall did not know was that Fort Erie had already fallen and what Norton had failed to see was the arrival of an additional 1,500 American soldiers and warriors from Fort Erie.

While Riall prepared to advance south toward the Americans, Norton and his warriors moved forward in advance of them with a handful of Canadian militia. From positions hidden in the woods, they harassed the American pickets, picking off dozens of soldiers. Annoyed, the American commander sent out a contingent of militia and warriors under Captain Peter B. Porter to eliminate the source of the harassment. Before they left the camp, the American Iroquois wound strips of white muslin around their heads to distinguish them from their Canadian cousins. When the American and Canadian-British Armies were within a mile of each other Norton's men split into three distinct groups. They hoped to continue to harass the Americans and perhaps eliminate some of the main force.

Captain Porter's force slipped into the forest to the south of the American encampment where they could not be seen by Norton's snipers. They proceed up both sides of the river until they surround one of Norton's groups. A fierce battle followed. According to Porter's account of the battle, the snipers immediately realized that they were outnumbered and resorted to the old tactic of withdrawing and regrouping. But their retreat was cut short by the American Iroquois, who pursued their Canadian cousins through the forest with chilling whoops. Few of the Canadians surrendered and Porter related that many turned suddenly to face their enemy and died bravely beneath the tomahawks of their brethren.

The chase ended abruptly when the American Iroquois encountered a second group of Canadian warriors lead by Norton himself. The Americans wheeled around to retreat from the larger force, stumbling over the carnage they'd created in the woods in their haste to get away. Norton's forces gave chase and more bodies, many with white kerchiefs tied to their heads, joined the carpet of dead on the forest floor. Norton's warriors were stunned by the sheer numbers of casualties. Eighty-seven warriors were killed within the space of a few moments. But with the enemy safely behind their own lines, Norton and his men could do little more than take up a position of support as the British met the Americans head on. Revenge would have to wait.

The Battle of Chippewa ended in a rout, with the British ceding the area to a much larger American force. But the battle had a devastating effect on the Iroquois. Disgusted by a conflict that was not truly theirs and had pit Iroquois against Iroquois, many withdrew. The Iroquois would no longer be a major force in the war. Norton himself would fight on with small groups of young warriors, but he would no longer enjoy the prestige and power he had had earlier in the war. When the war ended he went to England with his new wife and began work on a journal of his experiences. Shortly after its completion he resumed his wanderings. He was reportedly sighted at various points across North American until finally the sightings stopped. John Norton had disappeared. He was rumoured to have died in New Mexico in the 1830s but there is no proof.

Despite the tragic end to the war for the Iroquois and the somewhat inglorious end for Norton, both were credited for saving Upper Canada from an almost certain defeat in the first years of the war.

CHAPTER FOUR:
JAMES FITZGIBBON AND
THE BLOODY BOYS

Until the autumn of 1812 the war had not had much of an effect on the average citizen, so cross-border relations remained cordial. Canadian farmers in both Upper and Lower Canada continued selling their goods in American markets, and Vermont farmers supplied much of the beef consumed by British soldiers. Rationing was relatively new and not yet causing too much hardship. More importantly, the battles had mostly been confined to military installations and casualties had been light. That all changed after October 13, 1812.

Dozens of Canadian militiamen had fallen alongside Brock at the bloody Battle of Queenston Heights. In the following months, the Canadians and British would win one battle only to lose the next. Territory was gained and lost so often, and so rapidly, that the border became blurred. Soldiers who had become separated from their units roamed the frontier not knowing which side of the border they were on.

The people of Upper Canada were living in a perpetual battleground. Their farms were burned, their possessions looted, their men conscripted by the government or imprisoned by the enemy. This cruel reality forced even the most apathetic civilians to choose sides. Some sided with the Americans, but the majority stood firm as Canadians. The bravery of some of these civilians helped turn the tide of the war in Canada's favour. Lieutenant James FitzGibbon was fortunate enough to cross paths with two of these brave Canadians: Billy "The Scout" Green and Laura Secord.

Lieutenant James FitzGibbon was a self-educated man. Unlike many of his fellow officers in the British Army, he had earned his way through the ranks by recognition rather than through an exchange of coin. The son of a poor Irish

Civilian Life

As in most wars, civilians frequently suffered the worst depredations during the War of 1812. The men were conscripted or coerced into joining the militia, leaving their farms and homes defenceless against friend and foe alike. If the battles extended through the spring planting, entire communities faced the very real threat of famine during the winter months. But the immediate effects of living in a war zone could be just as devastating. Fields, like those belonging to John Chrysler's farm along the St. Lawrence River, served as impromptu battlegrounds, ensuring the loss of that year's crops and quite possibly the next year's too. Private homes were frequently commandeered to house troops or to serve as headquarters, and looting was commonplace as troops advanced and retreated over the same ground time and again.

While their fields were turned into battlegrounds and their homes into barracks for soldiers from both sides of the conflict, civilians were also forced to deal with shortages and rationing as the war continued. And what meagre supplies could be found were easily lost as both armies believed that civilians were charging inflated prices and occasionally felt justified in simply taking what they wanted. Fence posts became firewood, chicken coops were raided for eggs and meat, and gardens uprooted in search of vegetables. Livestock was carried off or butchered in the field. In 1813, General Francis de Rottenburg declared martial law in parts of the Niagara region, not because of any shortage but because the war-weary people of the region were refusing to furnish the soldiers with what they needed. The government was responsible for compensating those who lost property during the war but compensation was often as difficult to document as it as to secure. In fact, the majority of the numerous lawsuits launched by Canadians against British Army agents who had forcibly purchased supplies were dismissed by the courts. Very few civilians would recover everything they lost.

farmer, FitzGibbon joined the army at 17, sailing with Lord Nelson against Napoleon. Shortly after his arrival in Canada in 1813, at the age of 33, he attracted the attention of Major-General Brock. FitzGibbon had more than a hint of the brashness that was so much a part of Brock's character; the general recognized his potential and became his unofficial mentor. Brock helped the strong, ambitious FitzGibbon refine his manners and improve his diction, turning the soldier into a gentleman.

FitzGibbon was a natural leader, and easily earned the respect and loyalty of his men. He was so well respected that he was able to persuade his commanding officer, Brigadier General John Vincent, to allow him to form a special unit. FitzGibbon handpicked the men from the 49th Regiment and trained them vigorously in guerrilla warfare. They had one purpose: to chase down, capture, or kill the renegade American soldiers who were terrorizing the population of the Niagara frontier.

The elite unit quickly established a fierce reputation on both sides of the border. The grey-green coveralls they wore earned them the nickname "The Green Tigers." But they called themselves "The Bloody Boys," a name that stuck. They roamed the Niagara region on horseback, frequently in disguise, hunting the most notorious of the American invaders. Canadians loved the Bloody Boys. Stories of their escapades encouraged some of the bolder young men to help them harass the invading Americans. Even those who were less brave did what they could to help FitzGibbon and his men.

In April 1813, American warships sailed across Lake Ontario. The soldiers invaded and destroyed Fort York, then went on to loot the town of York. A month later, they turned their attention back to the south and began another vigorous attack on the Niagara frontier. Their first foray was a successful attack on Fort George, where FitzGibbon was stationed.

The young lieutenant, along with 1,400 other men and their commander, John Vincent, were forced to abandon the fort. They marched inland toward Beaver Dams, where they were joined by other British troops escaping from both Fort Erie, at the southern end of the Niagara frontier, and Amherstburg on the western frontier. With retreat the only option, Vincent sent the militia back to their homes. It made little sense to continue to house and feed a volunteer army during a retreat, especially when many of them were needed at home on their farms.

The Americans chased the retreating British for four weeks. The militia, and indeed most of the population of the Niagara Peninsula, had every reason to believe that the British were abandoning them. In fact, Vincent had been ordered to abandon the peninsula. His superiors considered it to be both indefensible and expendable. It had originally been deemed important only because it served as a buffer between the Americans and Kingston, the capital of Upper Canada. Fortunately for the people of Niagara, Vincent was not willing to give up the area without a fight.

Once the troops were off the peninsula, Vincent halted his retreat and set up camp at Burlington Heights. The British, now barely 1,600 men strong, were about to face a force of nearly 3,000 Americans. They needed an edge, and the daring James FitzGibbon was just the man to provide it.

On the morning of June 5, FitzGibbon dressed himself as a butter peddler. He made his way back along the peninsula to the American encampment near Stoney Creek, a village about 16 kilometres from the Canadian and British position. While selling his butter, he surreptitiously counted men and armaments. When he returned to his own camp, FitzGibbon was able to report that the Americans were disorganized and their men and guns were badly positioned. He had also found out that the Americans were expecting reinforcements to arrive soon. He advised Vincent to attack immediately.

While FitzGibbon had been reconnoitering in the American camp, two young farmers — Billy Green and his brother Levi — were innocently roaming the woods on the Niagara Escarpment, high above him. The last thing they expected to see on their morning walk was the American Army.

The Green family had moved to Canada from the United States 19 years earlier, just before Billy's birth. Until that day, Billy's sole claim to fame was that he was the first white child born in Stoney Creek. He was about to make another claim. The brothers were not interested in the position or strength of the army, but they were not about to pass up the chance to have a little fun. Hidden in deep foliage, they watched as the American advance guard marched by on the way to attack the British in Burlington Heights. The boys began whooping like warriors, terrorizing the American soldiers. They laughed silently as the stragglers at the end of the column broke into a run to catch up to the rest of the troop. "I tell you those simple fellows did run,"[1] Billy recounted years later.

When the coast was clear, Billy and Levi made their way to the village, crossing the road the American troops had just marched along. They came across a lone American soldier who was winding a rag around his bootless foot. The American reached for his gun, but Levi was quicker. He grabbed a stick and struck the soldier. When the other soldiers heard their comrade's yells, they begin firing. Billy and Levi disappeared into the woods and ran back up the escarpment. The brothers reached Levi's cabin safely. By then, a crowd of settlers, drawn by the sound of war whoops and gunfire, had come out onto the ridge to see what was happening. Billy and Levi joined them. They watched as the Americans traipsed through the village. Unable to resist a repeat performance, Billy whooped again and Levi answered him. One of the Americans fired at the hill, narrowly missing Levi's wife, Tina, and their infant daughter.

Billy and Levi hid in the woods while Tina retreated to the safety of a nearby trapper's hut. A group of soldiers knocked at the trapper's door and asked the terrified woman if she had seen any Natives. In a trembling voice, she told them a fierce band was roaming the mountain. The soldiers were convinced. Once the Americans had gone, Billy went to Stoney Creek to check on his sister, Keziah Corman, and her husband, Isaac. Keziah told him that Isaac had been arrested for answering insolently when the Americans asked for directions. Billy ran through the village and into the woods in search of his brother-in-law, whistling like a bird as he ran. Finally his whistles were answered by an owl hoot. It was Isaac.

Isaac had made his escape by pretending he was sympathetic to the American cause. He told the commander he was from Kentucky and was a first cousin to William Henry Harrison, the American governor of Indian Lands. It was a truthful statement; his mother was Harrison's aunt. The commander promptly released Isaac and gave him the password so the soldiers would allow him through their lines.

Isaac had sworn not to give the password to the British — so he did not. He gave it to Billy instead. Billy, caught up in the excitement and committed to do-ing his part for Canada, borrowed a horse and started out for Burlington Heights to give the precious information to the British. He rode the horse until it was exhausted, then walked the rest of the way. Billy arrived late that night, just as Vincent was preparing to attack. A night attack was extraordinary for an army that normally fought by traditional rules of war, but the situation called for drastic action. Darkness would be their ally; surprise their only hope.

Vincent had intelligence that the American cavalry would soon catch up with the infantry and they would then be in position to attack. The British had neither the arms nor the manpower to stage a frontal attack, and they could not withstand a frontal attack from the Americans. To make things worse, the British commanders believed American warships would arrive any day.

That night, young Billy proved to be much more than a good-luck charm to the British. Although they initially suspected him of being a spy, they eventually believed his story and took him to Vincent's commanding officer, Lieutenant-Colonel John Harvey. Billy gave him the password and told him where and how the Americans were camped. Harvey asked Billy if he could lead them. When the lad gave him an enthusiastic yes, the officer gave him a corporal's sword and told him to take the lead.

Billy galloped off toward Stoney Creek. Occasionally he grew frustrated with the soldiers lagging behind him and went back to urge them to move more quickly. It would be daylight soon, he cajoled. That would be soon enough to be killed, one of the men replied angrily.

They reached the encampment just before dawn on June 6, 1813. Billy dispatched one sentry with his knife, but another guard managed to fire a shot, alerting his fellow soldiers. The British dashed forward, whooping like warriors while firing their muskets. The Americans met them, and the line of battle swung madly. In the blackness, British and Americans retreated and advanced, and enemies become indistinguishable from allies. On the left, the British line faltered until FitzGibbon rode up and down restoring order. During the melee, two American generals were captured and the cannons were disabled. The American line broke and the troops scattered in retreat.

Gage House on the battlefield of Stoney Creek.

Major-General Vincent, who had been eager to lead his troops against the Americans, did not witness this victory. He became separated from his men before the battle started and was soon lost. He wandered through the thick forest as the battle raged, sure that his forces had been defeated. Two soldiers found him the next morning — minus his hat and his dignity.

Some days later, when Harvey wrote his official account of the Battle of Stoney Creek, June 6, 1813, he made no mention of the hapless Vincent's misfortune, nor did he mention the brave adventurer Billy Green. But in Stoney Creek, Billy became a folk hero, known throughout the region as "The Scout."

Richard Pierpont was 16 years old when he was captured in his native Senegal and sold as a slave to a British officer stationed in New York. When the Revolutionary War broke out, Pierpont was one of many slaves who were awarded their freedom in exchange for military service against the Americans. He served with distinction with Butler's Rangers and when the war ended, Pierpont fled to Canada as one of many Black Loyalists.

Slavery was still legal in the American colonies and Pierpont and his fellow Black Loyalists stood to lose more than most if the American invasion in 1812 proved successful. So, the 60-year-old Pierpont, and many other Black Loyalists, rushed to offer their services. A Coloured Corps was formed and its soldiers saw action in Queenston Heights alongside Major-General Brock.

On the morning of May 25, Pierpont was stationed with the rest of the coloured corps on the beach outside of Fort George. The Americans had been shelling the fort and beach for most of the morning and a thick fog had settled in. The American invasion force could not be far behind. As explosions rent the air, Pierpont and the others peered through the fog hoping to catch sight of the Americans. No one believed they would land at the beach. The British commander, General John Vincent, expected the invasion to arrive somewhere along the Niagara River and had concentrated the bulk of his force there.

As the bows of the first ships finally emerged from the fog, it quickly became clear that they were pointed directly at the beach. Realizing his error, Vincent quickly ordered his troops to the beach, but they were too late. As the massive American force landed, only the Coloured Corps and a few of the Fencibles were there to meet it. They bravely fixed bayonets and charged the boats, knowing that they had to stop the Americans from gaining a foothold on the beach if they were to have any chance of turning them back. But their efforts merely delayed the inevitable. The Coloured Corp and Fencibles held their ground much longer than they should have against the more numerous American troops, but were soon forced back up the hill and to the fort where they were met by Vincent. Within the hour, Vincent called for the complete abandonment of the fort.

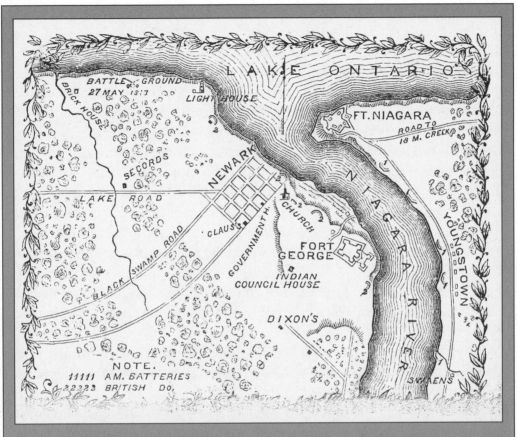

Benjamin Lossing's Field Book of the War of 1812.

The Coloured Corps, having lost many of their number on the beach, reluctantly joined the retreat. They would fight on in several other battles including the bloody battle of Lundy's Lane. When the war was over Pierpont and the remaining members of the Coloured Corps petitioned the government to allow them to return to their native Senegal. The government refused, instead encouraging them to integrate into Upper Canadian society by granting former members of the Coloured Guard parcels of land in the Niagara Region they had given so much to protect.

JAMES FITZGIBBON AND THE BLOODY BOYS

Upon their defeat at Stoney Creek, the Americans retreated to the safety of Fort George. After a hasty regrouping in their own camp, Vincent's troops followed the Americans. For three days they dogged the retreat. Luckily, they often came across wagonloads of supplies left behind by the fleeing Americans. Finally, the British and Canadians stood before the wooden palisades of the fort. They could not get in; the fort was too heavily defended. But nor could the Americans break out in any significant numbers. They did manage to make occasional raids on nearby farms and villages. One of the most infamous men in these raiding parties was Cyrenius Chapin, a doctor from Buffalo, New York. The doctor was well-known for his ruthless plundering of the homes of local settlers. FitzGibbon was disgusted by Chapin's rampages and was determined to put an end to them — the Irishman had come to love Canada and wanted to protect the civilians. He knew Chapin was in the fort. He was just waiting for a chance to capture him.

That chance came on June 19. FitzGibbon heard that the doctor had slipped out of the fort with a raiding party, so he and his Bloody Boys began scouring the Niagara Peninsula looking for Chapin. They had tracked the raiding party to the countryside around the village of Lundy's Lane, almost halfway down the peninsula. FitzGibbon, believing he would attract less attention on his own, told his men to wait outside the village.

On the road into the village, the wife of a local militiaman waved him down and told him that Chapin was just ahead with more than 200 men. She urged FitzGibbon to flee to safety. But retreat was not something FitzGibbon was prepared to do. His enemy was near — he was not about to let him go. FitzGibbon spotted a horse that belonged to one of the raiders tied to a post outside a tavern. He went into the tavern and was immediately accosted by two raiders — one of whom levelled a rifle at him. The brash FitzGibbon extended a hand to the American and moved toward him in a friendly manner, as if he had recognized him as an acquaintance. This action confused the American for just long enough to allow FitzGibbon to seize the rifle and order him to surrender. The other American took aim, but FitzGibbon grabbed his rifle before he could fire.

The DeCou homestead, Fitzgibbon's headquarters.

During the ensuing struggle, the three men tumbled out of the tavern. The woman who had warned FitzGibbon about the raiders was still on the road. She pleaded for help from several passing wagons, but the drivers did not want to get involved. Only a small boy answered her plea by throwing stones at the Americans. One of the raiders grabbed hold of FitzGibbon's sword. This could have been the end of FitzGibbon but for the innkeeper's plucky wife. The woman had rushed outside to watch the fight, still holding her baby. When she saw FitzGibbon's plight, she put the baby down, ran forward, and kicked the sword from the

American's hand. Within seconds she had scooped up her baby and disappeared into the tavern. Finally, the innkeeper arrived and helped FitzGibbon disarm and arrest the Americans.

Chapin, who must have been somewhere nearby, escaped.

A few days later, Vincent ordered FitzGibbon to take up residence at the De-Cou homestead near Beaver Dams. It was on the escarpment, about 30 kilometres southwest of Fort George. The house was to be the headquarters for FitzGibbon and the Bloody Boys while they scouted the countryside looking for American troops who might have slipped out of Fort George.

Meanwhile, the Americans trapped inside the fort grew increasingly frustrated at not being able to break free and renew their campaign. They were also frustrated with FitzGibbon and his Bloody Boys, who had been a nuisance for long enough. American spies had informed the incarcerated Americans that FitzGibbon had been sent to the DeCou homestead to set up patrols. The commander at the fort sent out a message for more troops to come to their aid. The plan was that the troops would attack the hated FitzGibbon first, and then go on to the fort and break through the line of soldiers and warriors holding siege. The rescuing troops, led by Lieutenant-Colonel Charles Boerstler, were soon on their way.

A small advance party of Boerstler's men stopped in Queenston to wait for the rest of the force. They chose a house at random and demanded that the residents serve them dinner. They had chosen the home of Laura Ingersoll Secord.

Laura Secord and her husband, James, were both the children of United Empire Loyalists. Their families had fled to Canada during the American War of Independence almost 40 years before. James owned a shop and the family was fairly prosperous. When war had been declared, James had joined the militia. At that time, the war had seemed distant. That was before October 1812 and the Battle of Queenston Heights, when the war had come to their doorstep — literally. During that battle, Laura and her children sheltered at a farm outside the village while James stayed to fight. When she and the children returned, James was nowhere to be found. She went to the battlefield to find him. The tiny woman struggled through the mud and bloodstained leaves, past the dead and wounded until, finally, she found him. He had been shot in the kneecap and shoulder and was in grave condition. Laura begged the help of a passing soldier and together they got James home. James lived, but his war service was over.

Even though no more battles were being fought in Queenston, American soldiers frequently looted the homes. Occasionally, they burned them to the ground. By the time Boerstler's men burst into the Secord home on June 21, 1813, it had already been raided twice. The first time, Laura had protected the family heirloom, a rare collection of Spanish doubloons, by tossing them into a boiling cauldron of water hanging over the kitchen fire. The second time, according to some accounts, one of the American soldiers had boasted that once they had chased away the British, he would return to claim the Secord property as his own. Laura was infuriated by the arrogance of the American. She told him that the only land in Queenstown he would ever be able to claim as his own would be a six-foot grave. His companions returned later that day and told Laura that her prediction had proved true: the man had been killed in a skirmish with Canadian soldiers.

Now, with this third invasion of her home, the feisty 38-year-old was justifiably incensed. She reluctantly agreed to the soldiers' demand for dinner. With her husband still in bed recovering from his wounds, and no Canadian militia nearby, she had no choice. As the evening wore on, the Americans grew bolder, bragging that they were planning a surprise attack on FitzGibbon at the DeCou homestead. They also talked about their grand plans to open up the entire peninsula to a massive American attack. Laura had no details of how or when the attack would take place, but she knew that FitzGibbon was Canada's best chance for holding Niagara. She also knew that he had to be warned. Her husband was too severely injured to make the 30-kilometre journey to the DeCou home. She made up her mind to find another way to warn FitzGibbon.

The next day dawned blistering hot. Laura rose early and put on a long cotton dress and white bonnet. Light slippers with low heels covered her feet. They would not offer much protection on her journey, but they would not raise any suspicion among the Americans. Laura did not want to be caught — the penalty for spying was death by firing squad. As dawn broke, she set out for her sister-in-law's home in the nearby village of St. David's, a small basket of preserves in hand. Along the way, Laura was stopped twice by American patrols. She told them that she was going to visit her ailing brother in St. David's. This part of her story was true; Charles Ingersoll was indeed recuperating from a fever. The soldiers knew this, so they let her pass.

Laura was hoping that if her brother was too ill to go to FitzGibbon, one of her older nephews would go instead. When she got to St. David's later that morning, she found that Charles was still feverish. Worse still, the boys had both joined the Canadian militia. She knew she had to make the 25-kilometre journey herself. According to some sources, Laura's niece accompanied her as far as Shipman's Corners, where the young woman collapsed from exhaustion.

Laura walked on the road as far as the village of Shipman's Corners, then travelled cross-country to avoid American patrols. She waded through a vast, treacherous quagmire known as Black Swamp, an area that teemed with rattlesnakes and was home to wolves and wildcats. She toiled across the swamp all afternoon, suffering terribly from the heat. Her courage almost failed her when she heard one, then several wolf howls. By the time she reached the edge of the swamp, it was early evening. She was ragged, shoeless, and exhausted, but she still had a long way to go.

As Laura climbed up a steep escarpment, she realized she was being watched. Still, she forged ahead through the thick brush. At the edge of a clearing, she found herself surrounded by a group of Caughnawaga warriors. Once the shaken woman discovered they were loyal to the British, she tried to explain the situation to the chief and make him understand the urgency of her mission. The chief sent two warriors to escort the bedraggled Laura to FitzGibbon. They arrived at the DeCou house just before midnight. Laura had been walking for almost 18 hours.

Laura told the amazed FitzGibbon all she knew, and then collapsed. FitzGibbon gently revived her and told his officers to escort her to the nearby farm of her friend, a Miss Tournay. There, Laura slept for 22 hours straight.

FitzGibbon acted on Laura's information immediately. He sent the Caughnawaga warriors to watch for the American advance, and then made his own preparations to leave. The grateful lieutenant marvelled at the courage of this

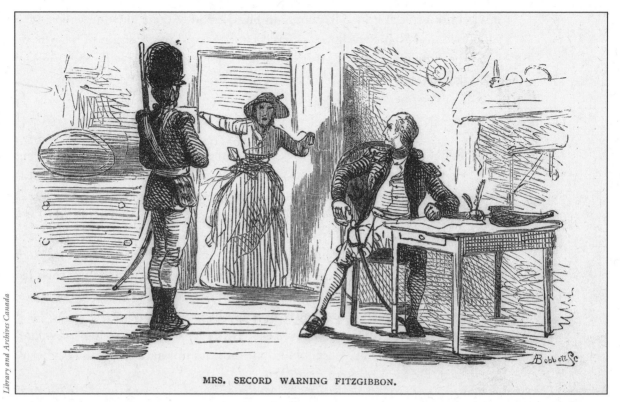

MRS. SECORD WARNING FITZGIBBON.

Laura Secord warning Fitzgibbon.

seemingly fragile woman. Years later he wrote, "I have ever since held myself personally indebted to her for her conduct upon that occasion."[2]

During that long, terrible day, Laura's husband had been sick with worry. He had no idea if she had made it through the American lines or whether she had been captured. When she returned home, neither of them spoke openly of her journey. There were American sympathizers in the village. If these people found out she had warned FitzGibbon, they would tell the Americans.

After the war, Laura broke her silence about her brave walk in order to get some compensation from the British. James had lost his shop and was unable to find work because of his war injuries. The family was destitute. Laura sent numerous petitions to the Prince Regent, and FitzGibbon wrote a glowing letter in her support. Local politicians finally offered James Secord the position of magistrate, which he gratefully accepted. In 1860, when Laura was 83 years old, the Prince of Wales granted her a reward of £100.

— — — —

At midnight on June 22, 1813, Boerstler and the rest of his men reached Queenston. He put patrols in place to ensure that no citizen escaped to warn the British. He was, of course, unaware that this was a useless precaution. At daybreak on June 23, the Americans marched to St. David's. Eleven hours later, they ran into two Caughnawaga scouts. They shot one, but the other escaped and warned François Ducharme, their French Canadian commander. Ducharme, in turn, sent scouts to warn FitzGibbon that the Americans had arrived. Ducharme then led his several hundred warriors in an attack on the Americans, who were perched on the Niagara Escarpment along a narrow strip of land lined on both sides by dense forest. The area was known as Beaver Dams. The Americans were just a few kilometres from their quarry, FitzGibbon, but they did not have to go any farther to get to him. He went to them instead.

Ducharme's Caughnawagas, supported by several dozen Mohawks, fired from the forest. Boerstler's troops returned fire but soon used up their ammunition. The heavy fire from the forests showed no sign of letting up, and the exhausted soldiers knew they were vulnerable.

Meanwhile, FitzGibbon had been concealed in the forest, waiting for his reinforcements to arrive before he joined the fight. FitzGibbon had only 44 Bloody Boys with him. Although the reinforcements were nowhere in sight, he knew he had to act. He decided on an audacious bluff. With his customary aplomb, he walked out carrying a white flag and demanded that Boerstler surrender. He told the American that the British had his troops completely surrounded. He also added the now familiar falsehood that the Native warriors would massacre the Americans unless they surrendered immediately. Boerstler, not surprisingly, refused. He was not prepared to surrender to an army he had not even seen.

Carrying his bluff one stage further, FitzGibbon suggested that the Americans send an officer to inspect the strength of the British troops. Then FitzGibbon strode back into the forest on the pretext of asking his superior's permission to allow an American officer to see the troops. FitzGibbon's bluff would have been exposed if it had not been for an incredible piece of luck. His hastily hatched plan was to get a British officer in full uniform to pose as his superior. But he did not have a single British officer in his party.

While he was desperately trying to come up with another plan, the advance party of his reinforcements came crashing through the forest. The relieved FitzGibbon quickly ordered one of the British officers to play the role of the commanding officer. The officer, a man named John Hall, obediently accompanied FitzGibbon back out into the clearing. When the American officer asked Hall to show his troops, the British soldier drew himself up and haughtily declared that it would be humiliating to display his force to the Americans. He assured the officer that it was large enough to annihilate Boerstler's forces.

Hearing this report, Boerstler asked for time to decide. FitzGibbon gave him five minutes, and again used the lie that he would not be able to control the Native warriors for longer than that. Boerstler threw up his hands and begged to be saved from the warriors.

The outrageous bluff had worked, but FitzGibbon faced another hurdle. He had to figure out how to disarm 500 Americans with only his band of Bloody Boys, a handful of warriors, and a dozen Dragoons. Surrenders were usually very formal, with the surrendering army literally handing their weapons to their captors. Of course, FitzGibbon could not allow this. If the Americans realized how small a group they had surrendered to, they would call off the surrender and continue the fight.

While FitzGibbon was pondering his next move, his real commanding officer finally arrived with a small contingent of soldiers. As FitzGibbon's superior, it was the commanding officer's prerogative to oversee the surrender. Unfortunately, he did not listen to FitzGibbon's concern about the Americans seeing their meagre numbers. He told Boerstler to march his troops between the British troops, laying their weapons on the ground. FitzGibbon, ever quick-witted, asked — in an unnaturally loud voice — if it was really a good idea to march the Americans past the still angry warriors. The Americans immediately tossed down their weapons.

When writing his report of the Battle of Beaver Dams, June 23, 1813, FitzGibbon gave much of the credit to the Caughnawaga warriors. "With respect to the affair with Boerstler, not a shot was fired on our side by any but the Indians. They beat the American detachment into a state of terror; and the only share I claim is taking advantage of a favourable moment to offer them protection from the tomahawk and scalping knife."[3]

The Caughnawaga suffered 15 deaths and 25 wounded that day. Unfortunately, the Mohawks took most of the spoils, leaving the Caughnawaga with next to nothing. John Norton, the Mohawk chief, later observed, "... the Caughnawaga fought the battle, the Mohawks got the plunder and FitzGibbon got the credit."[4] For the courage and ingenuity he had shown at the Battle of Beaver Dams, James FitzGibbon was promoted to the rank of captain.

A few weeks after the victory at Beaver Dams, FitzGibbon and 40 Bloody Boys crossed the Niagara River to raid the American supply depot of Black Rock. Just as FitzGibbon was about to launch the raid, a British force of about 200 regulars arrived. Their commander, Cecil Bishopp, had also planned to attack the supply depot, but he was worried he might not have enough men. When FitzGibbon heard this, he threw his head back and laughed.

The two groups joined forces and successfully raided the depot. FitzGibbon was ready to make a quick getaway, but Bishopp delayed their departure to load 40 barrels of much-needed salt onto his boat. During that short time, American reinforcements arrived. In the ensuing fight, Bishopp and several of his soldiers were fatally wounded.

More than a year later, in August 1814, FitzGibbon took part in the long, bloody siege of Fort Erie. In three months, the British had made three attempts to breech the walls of the fort. Each time, they had been driven back by the American gunners. The British succeeded on the fourth attempt, but reached only one of the fort's inner bastions. The British soldiers were discouraged and pessimistic about the outcome of the siege.

During this trying time, FitzGibbon requested permission to go to Kingston to get married. Permission was granted and he set off, promising to be back within three days. It seemed a strange request in the middle of a battle but, as always, FitzGibbon had a purpose.

"There was a little girl I loved," he wrote to a friend, "and I knew that if I could but marry her before I was killed, and I a captain, she would have the pension of a captain's widow."[5] He married his sweetheart on August 14, then left her on the church steps to return to a battle he did not expect to survive.

FitzGibbon did survive the battle of Fort Erie. Many other British soldiers were not as lucky. The toll was 366 killed or wounded, and 539 taken prisoner or listed as missing. Against all odds, the gallant Irishman survived the entire war without serious injury. He returned to his wife, and they made their home in the country he had fought for and loved. When his wife died in 1846, FitzGibbon retired to England, where he was made a Knight of Windsor for his services to the Crown.

The old soldier longed to return to Canada, but he had duties that kept him in England. He wrote to a former comrade who still lived in Canada, "I sometimes exclaim 'Thank God, I have Canada to fall back upon.' Its future seems to me more full of promise than any other section of the human family. I long to be among you."[6]

CHAPTER FIVE:
TECUMSEH

Brock fought in defence of the British Empire, and FitzGibbon fought to protect the Canadian colony he had grown to love. Another of their allies, the great chief Tecumseh, championed a third cause: that of the Native peoples.

No one felt the loss of Brock as keenly as the renowned Shawnee chief. The two shared a peculiar relationship. Both men were courageous, impetuous, and unwaveringly loyal to their cause. They were united by a shared goal — the defeat of the Americans — but neither man completely trusted the other. And if Brock was willing to use Tecumseh and the Native warriors to win the war for the British, Tecumseh was equally willing to use the British to pursue his own vision of a United Native Empire.

Tecumseh was born in the Ohio Territories around 1768. His father had been killed in a battle with the settlers when Tecumseh was just six years old. His older brother, Cheesuaka, took responsibility for the young Tecumseh, training him to be both a warrior and a leader. He also trained him to distrust the settlers, although that was hardly necessary. During his youth, Tecumseh watched the American government take more and more land from his people. This made him resentful. When Cheesuaka died a violent death at the hands of whites, Tecumseh became dangerously bitter.

As an adult, Tecumseh warned his fellow peoples, "The white men aren't friends to the Indians … at first they only asked for land sufficient for a wigwam; now, nothing will satisfy them but the whole of our hunting grounds from the rising to the setting sun."[1] Tecumseh had participated in his first battle at the age of 15 and quickly earned a reputation as a courageous and ruthless warrior. But he was also compassionate. While still a young man, he watched a white prisoner being burned to death at the stake. He swore he would never again allow such atrocities in his presence.

When the war began, Tecumseh was 44 years old. He was, by most accounts, a well-built man with handsome features, copper skin, and clear hazel eyes. When wearing war paint and brandishing a tomahawk, he looked as fearsome as the most ferocious warrior, but when delivering one of his eloquent speeches to the settlers, either in English or Shawnee, he appeared as dignified and composed as any British officer. No authentic likeness exists of Tecumseh because he refused to have his portrait painted. However, a wonderful description, written by one of Brock's aides, paints a picture of its own.

> Three small silver crowns, or coronets, were suspended from the lower cartilage of his aquiline nose; and a large silver medallion of George III ... was attached to a mixed coloured wampum string, and hung around his neck. His dress consisted of a plain, neat uniform, tanned deerskin jacket, with long trousers of the same material, the seams of both being covered with neatly cut fringe; and he had on his feet leather moccasins, much ornamented with work made from the dyed quills of the porcupine.[2]

— — — —

Not much is known about Tecumseh's personal life other than he eschewed liquor and, after being married four times, eventually chose to live without women in his life. Legend has it that between wives he fell in love with the 16-year-old daughter of a settler. It is said she taught him English and introduced him to the Bible and Shakespeare — his favourite play was Hamlet. The girl said she would marry him if he agreed to renounce his Indian ways and live as a white man. He refused. Whether the story has any foundation in fact or not, by the time war broke out between Canada and the United States in June 1812, he was a man with only one passion: his cause.

His cause was clear and noble. He dreamed of an "Indian Nation" stretching from the Great Lakes to the Gulf of Mexico. He dreamed of uniting the First Nations in a confederation similar to that of the United States. If anyone was capable of achieving this, it was Tecumseh. The brilliant tactician and gifted orator managed to convince many of the Native leaders to support his vision — but not all. The British got their first glimpse of the charismatic Tecumseh in 1810, when they invited him to Fort Amherstburg to meet Matthew Elliott, the Indian Department representative. Elliott had been charged with the task of finding out whether the Shawnee and other groups would be loyal to the British if war broke out with the Americans.

Elliott was a Loyalist who had come to Canada after the American War of Independence. He spent a lot of time with the Native peoples, and he respected them. He had expected Tecumseh to be lukewarm about the idea of supporting the British. He was surprised, and pleased, when Tecumseh declared his willingness to fight the Americans. Tecumseh made it clear that he had no interest in the quarrels between white people, but would willingly strike at the Americans if they continued to encroach on his land. For several years, Tecumseh and his younger brother had been travelling among the different Native peoples in the United States and Upper and Lower Canada, encouraging the nations to join the cause. They were persuasive men. By 1811, more than 1,000 warriors had left their homes to join the brothers in an inter-tribal settlement at the confluence of the Tippecanoe and Wabash Rivers.

Tecumseh's brother was a mystic known to the settlers and Natives alike as the Prophet. He was the group's spiritual leader, preaching that the encroachment of the settlers was a test from the Great Spirit. He maintained that the Native peoples must return to their old way of life or risk losing everything. He was feared by the whites but revered by his people. The settlement was dubbed Prophet's Town. But for political and military leadership, the warriors and the Prophet turned to Tecumseh, who wanted to avoid bloodshed but was willing to use force if his words failed to stop the sale of land to the Americans. Tecumseh threatened to kill any chief who sold more land to the settlers.

In the summer of 1811, several chiefs sold portions of their land to the Americans. The deals were brokered by the governor of Indian Lands, William Henry Harrison. The governor was well aware that Tecumseh and his brother would be furious and would likely harass the settlers on the recently purchased land. In an attempt to placate the brothers, Harrison invited them to a meeting at his estate near the town of Vincennes, Indiana.

Harrison, a shrewd man, thought out his strategy carefully. He summoned the chiefs who had sold the land and, as an added precaution, called up a large contingent of soldiers to stand guard and ensure his safety. Planning to intimidate Tecumseh, the governor would be seated on a raised dais, and Tecumseh and his men would be seated on the ground below him. Harrison had everything arranged to his satisfaction by the scheduled date of the meeting. Then he waited, and waited some more.

Tecumseh finally arrived on July 27 — three days late — and not with the small escort he had been asked to bring, but with 300 heavily armed warriors. As Harrison would quickly learn, Tecumseh was not easily intimidated. He refused to sit below Harrison and, ignoring the general's intricate staging, Tecumseh sat on the ground some distance away, forcing Harrison to come to him. Addressing the chiefs and Harrison, Tecumseh thundered that the chiefs had no right to sell the land because it belonged to all Native peoples. "Sell a country!" he exclaimed. "Why not sell the air, the clouds, and the great sea, as well as the earth? Did not Great Spirit make them all for the use of his children?"[3]

Tecumseh was so angry that the assembly feared he would loose his warriors on Harrison. But the warriors were held in check. Following Tecumseh's passionate speech, they turned and thundered away on their war ponies, leaving Harrison nervous, vexed, and impressed. In a report to his government, Harrison wrote, "If it were not for the vicinity of the United States, [Tecumseh] would, perhaps, be the founder of an empire that would rival in glory Mexico and Peru. No difficulties deter him. For years he has been in constant motion. You see him today on the Wabash and in a short time hear of him on the shores of Lake Erie or Michigan, or on the banks of the Mississippi, and wherever he goes he makes an impression favourable to his purposes. He is now upon the last round to put a finishing stroke to his work."[4]

During the next two months, Harrison alternately fumed and worried as more Native people flocked to Tecumseh and his brother at Prophet's Town. Tecumseh continued travelling across the continent, seeking to unite the scattered Native peoples. Finally, in the fall of 1811, Harrison made his move. While Tecumseh was in the southern states, Harrison had a fort built in the Indiana territory that Tecumseh and the Prophet had refused to yield. It was a show of force, but Harrison was also clearly trying to lure the impetuous Prophet into battle while his more cautious brother was not around to control him.

In late October, Harrison began marching his army toward Prophet's Town. On November 11, 1811, justifiably convinced the Americans were coming to destroy the settlement, the Prophet launched a pre-emptive attack against the Americans. Harrison's troops fought them off easily. This show of American military strength made many of the Native warriors think twice about their allegiance to the brothers. Several hundred went back to their own lands, never to return to the cause. Others abandoned the settlement but regrouped somewhere safer. Within two days of the Battle of Tippecanoe, Prophet's Town was completely deserted. Harrison's soldiers rode in and razed it to the ground, taking care to destroy all of the settlement's cooking implements and stores of food so that they would be unable to last the winter if they did choose to return.

When Tecumseh returned from his journey to find Prophet's Town in ruins and his followers scattered, he swore vengeance on Harrison and all his kind. The Americans sent envoy after envoy to Tecumseh in an effort to win him over, but the die had been cast. Tecumseh had decided to throw in his lot with the British. He sent runners to inform all the First Nations of his decision. Twelve responded, each sending two political chiefs and two war chiefs. By May of 1812, Tecumseh had recruited another 600 men. They waited patiently for the war to begin.

By the time war was declared, Tecumseh had already been tracking American movements and reporting them to the British. One of his quarries was Brigadier General William Hull, the unlucky soldier whose mail had been intercepted when the British captured the *Cuyahoga Packet* on June 21, 1812. In July, Hull had crossed into Upper Canada from Fort Detroit and taken the village of Sandwich on Canada's western frontier. His next target was the nearby Fort Amherstburg. He was not sure if he had enough men to take the fort, so he decided to send out bands of militia to test the strength of the British. Tecumseh and his warriors were watching.

Why War?

The War Hawks in the U.S. Congress sited a long list of grievances that they felt justified an attack on Canada. Chief among these was Britain's determination to break the U.S. trade relationship with Britain's enemy, France. The restrictions placed upon U.S. trade virtually ended America's economic contact with France and, by extension, with all of continental Europe, since at that time Napoleon controlled almost the entire European continent.

Britain's chief instrument for controlling trade was its massive navy. Such a large navy needed an equally large number of sailors. Since pay and conditions on board naval ships tended to be less than ideal, desertions were commonplace. Many of the deserters took refuge in the United States. To counteract the loss, the British would frequently stop American Merchant Marine ships, looking for British deserters. The Americans argued that the deserters were American citizens and had a right to choose where they wanted to live. The British disagreed and impressed the men back into the navy. Additionally, they declared that any British-born American could be impressed.

The third irritant for the War Hawks was Britain's perceived involvement in the United States's battles for control of the west and the Native American tribes who lived there. Many of the settlers and many Congress members believed that the British were arming and funding the Native Americans and actively undermining U.S. interests in the region.

On June 12, President Madison stood up in the House of Representatives and detailed a long list of U.S. grievances against Britain. When he was done, the representatives quickly voted to declare war. A few days later, General Hull and his army were on their way to Detroit and the Cuyahoga Packet *was taken.*

When the militia were halfway between Sandwich and Fort Amherstburg, Tecumseh's warriors swooped down on them. The men were terrified. Against the orders of their officers, they retreated. When the officers threatened to shoot the deserters, they told them they would rather be shot by one of their own than killed by the warriors. Tecumseh, along with British and Canadian troops, upset Hull's plans farther. On August 5, 1812, they crossed the border into Brownstown, Michigan, and attacked a wagon train carrying provisions for Hull's army.

TECUMSEH

This disaster, combined with the news that Brock's troops had captured Fort Michilimackinac, prompted Hull to withdraw his troops from Canadian soil and return to Fort Detroit. But even there he was not safe from Tecumseh.

The warriors lurked in the dense woods between Brownstown and Fort Detroit, waiting for another wagon train of supplies. It soon arrived. As the soldiers guarding the convoy passed Brownstone, they saw the impaled corpses of their fallen comrades from the battle the week before. Tecumseh had left them there in an effort to intimidate the Americans. It worked. In the battle that followed, the Americans were once again routed.

After that battle, Tecumseh returned to Fort Amherstburg, where he had his first meeting with General Brock and aligned himself with the British general, whom Tecumseh would be proud to follow into battle. Within a few days, Tecumseh and his warriors played a strategic role in the bloodless capture of Hull's troops and Fort Detroit.

After the capture, Hull, who lived out the rest of his days in disgrace, blamed Tecumseh and his warriors for his defeat. Surprisingly, Brock failed to mention Tecumseh in his official correspondence about the fall of Detroit, though in a later correspondence he admitted that losing the allegiance of Tecumseh could prove fatal to the war. In that same correspondence, Brock reminded the British political leaders of their promise to support a Native confederation south of the Great Lakes. Tecumseh saw that Brock was keeping his word and for awhile that, and a string of Canadian victories, was enough.

Tecumseh was also a man of his word. He demonstrated that at the surrender of Fort Detroit by keeping his promise to prevent a massacre. He was also compassionate. Stories of his acts of kindness circulated among the Canadians, British, and Americans and were retold in barracks and cabins on both sides of the border. One story involved an American minister captured at the surrender of Fort Detroit. Brock's deputy, Lieutenant-Colonel Henry Proctor, had been put in charge of the surrender. He was an officious man and was going to imprison the minister because he would not swear allegiance to the Crown. Tecumseh felt this was wrong and protested. Proctor ignored Tecumseh. Angry over this perceived injustice, the chief threatened to break his alliance with the British right then and there. Proctor reluctantly released the minister.

Another story involved a young American boy tending two oxen, whom Tecumseh happened upon. Tecumseh's men needed food, so he took the oxen but promised to compensate the family. However, when Tecumseh asked the Indian Department representative to pay for the oxen, Elliott declared the animals were spoils of war and refused to pay. An implacable and eventually successful Tecumseh insisted, and also demanded an extra dollar to pay for the boy's time and trouble in collecting payment.

At the beginning of August 1812, Tecumseh felt confident that his dream of a Native confederacy would soon be a reality. He was allied with the winning side and he had finally convinced Walk-in-Water, a Wyandot chief, to cross to the British side. This was of critical importance to Tecumseh's vision. The Wyandot were a senior nation. Where they went, others would surely follow. Then Tecumseh heard that the British governor general had negotiated a ceasefire. He was furious. His dream would never become a reality unless he could fight, and conquer, the Americans. Like Brock, Tecumseh knew that the British and Native peoples had to strike before the Americans had an opportunity to move more men and troops to the Niagara front or the western front.

Disgusted with his allies, Tecumseh left the battlefront and returned to the southern states to convince the Native peoples there to join his confederacy. The British did not see him again that winter. However, Tecumseh realized his fortunes were irrevocably tied to the British. He and his 2,000 men rejoined them at Amherstburg in the spring of 1813. There, he learned that Brock had been killed at Queenston Heights. It was a devastating blow. Tecumseh was sorry to lose a man he respected, but he was even more concerned about what Brock's death would mean for his dream of a Native confederacy. To add to his misery, Tecumseh knew he would have to give his allegiance to Brock's successor, Lieutenant-Colonel Henry Proctor — a man he had little use for. Proctor was not the commander his predecessor had been.

On January 19, 1813 — while Tecumseh was in the south — Proctor crossed the frozen Detroit River to launch a counterattack against the Americans who had taken the Canadian settlement of River Raisin. He was accompanied by Native warriors under the leadership of Roundhead, a Wyandot chief. The battle was short and savage. The British took 500 American prisoners, but the nervous Proctor almost immediately retreated to the relative safety of the village of Brownstown and left the American prisoners in the hands of Roundhead and his warriors.

The River Raisin Massacre

On January 22, 1813, an 1,100-strong force led by Colonel Henry Proctor attacked an American force under General James Winchester at the Raisin River Settlement in the Michigan territories. Winchester's men had become separated from the main American force and were completely unprepared when Proctor's men attacked.

The battle was short-lived and after securing a promise from Proctor regarding the safety of his men and the villagers, Winchester handed over his sword. Buoyed by his success, Proctor gave little thought to the terms of surrender and quickly ordered his troops to move on. He left a few guards behind to watch over the nearly 400 prisoners. They were also expected to secure treatment for the wounded Americans and arrange for sleds to take them out of the area. Neither materialized and the guards, anxious to join their brethren, soon abandoned the prisoners and the village. Unbeknownst to anyone, a group of 200 Seneca had turned back to the village, intent on seeking vengeance for their brethren who had been killed in battle.

The furious warriors looted and burned homes in the settlement and then turned their attention to the prisoners. In the massacre that ensued, it was said that the muddy Raisin River ran red with the blood of the murdered Americans and settlers. Accounts of the number of dead vary — some say as low as 30, some as high as hundreds, but regardless of the numbers the massacre marked a turning point in American opinions about the war. Fuelled by newspaper accounts of the massacre, "Remember the River Raisin!" became a rallying cry for the American militia. And the memories of that day were instrumental in spurring on the Kentucky militia as they chased Tecumseh up the Thames River.

CANADA ON FIRE

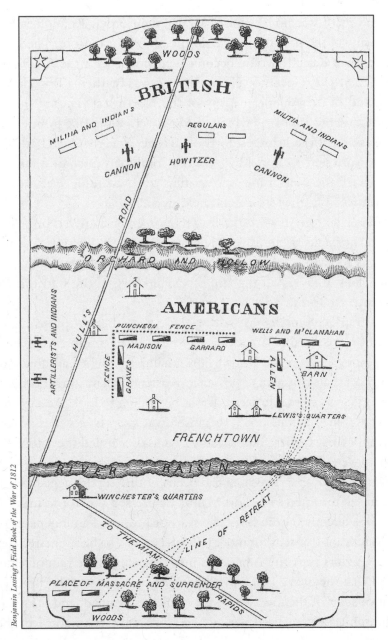

WOODS

BRITISH

MILITIA AND INDIANS

REGULARS

MILITIA AND INDIANS

CANNON

HOWITZER

CANNON

ROAD

ORCHARD AND HOLLOW

AMERICANS

ARTILLERISTS AND INDIANS

HULL'S

PUNCHEON FENCE

WELLS AND M'CLANAHAN

MADISON

GARRARD

FENCE

ALLEN

GRAVES

BARN

LEWIS'S QUARTERS

FRENCHTOWN

RIVER RAISIN

WINCHESTER'S QUARTERS

TO THE MIAMI

LINE OF RETREAT

RAPIDS

PLACE OF MASSACRE AND SURRENDER

WOODS

Benjamin Lossing's Field Book of the War of 1812

Battle of the River Raisin.

This time there was no Tecumseh to maintain order. Roundhead's warriors murdered many of the prisoners and held the others for ransom. Thereafter, "Remember the River Raisin!" would become a rallying cry for the American militia.

In October 1812, Governor Harrison, who was by then a Brigadier General, took command of the American Army of the Northwest. During the winter of 1812–13, he ordered a fort to be built at Meigs across the lake from Fort Amherstburg. It was one of the strongest forts of its time. In early May 1813, Tecumseh and Proctor were sent to Fort Meigs with a combined force of 3,000 men. Attempts to breach the walls using heavy artillery proved futile. Tecumseh and his men were restless, but they stayed and held siege.

A few days later, on May 5, American reinforcements arrived by boat. As they moved from the banks of the River Maumee to the fort, Tecumseh sent a handful of warriors to harass their flanks. With the massacre of River Raisin still fresh in the Americans' minds, half the reinforcements chased the warriors, following them deep into the forest.

It was a trap. Tecumseh was waiting there with the rest of his men. By the time the fight was over, 650 Americans had been killed or captured. The warriors marched the prisoners to the British Fort Miami. First the captured Americans were stripped of their clothes and possessions, then the harassment turned deadly, and several prisoners were murdered. It was beginning to look like a re-enactment of the River Raisin. But this time, Tecumseh was near. As soon as he found out what was happening, he berated his warriors and demanded they stop. The terrified prisoners were finally left alone.

Meanwhile, Proctor and his men had been continuing the siege of Fort Meigs. When Tecumseh returned from Fort Miami, he pressed Proctor to make a second attack, but not directly on the fort. The warrior proposed an ingenious plan. He knew the Americans had sent for more reinforcements, so he suggested the British and Native warriors trick the Americans into believing these reinforcements had arrived, and that they were being attacked. The warriors and the British soldiers moved out of sight of the fort, where they yelled, screamed, and fired their muskets. Tecumseh expected the Americans to leave the fort to come to the aid of their reinforcements, and when they did they would get a nasty surprise. The ploy almost worked. The men in the fort heard the sounds of a pitched battle and were anxious to engage, but their commander held them back. He suspected a trick.

Again, Tecumseh was frustrated and wanted to leave. Proctor, realizing he could not keep Tecumseh there any longer, withdrew his troops. During the next few weeks, Proctor and Tecumseh suffered a string of humiliating defeats. Dozens of Tecumseh's men deserted. A British victory — and Tecumseh's dreams — seemed to be slipping away. On September 10, 1813, British and American battleships waged a battle on Lake Erie. Proctor and Tecumseh watched from Fort Amherstburg while the British suffered their first naval defeat. Proctor, terrified of losing the Native alliance, tried to convince Tecumseh that the British had actually won the battle.

Tecumseh, of course, was no fool. He knew the British had been defeated, and he suspected they were planning to retreat. Retreating from his old enemy Harrison was unthinkable to the proud chief. He had no faith in Proctor, so he turned to Matthew Elliot, the Indian Department representative. Tecumseh told Elliot that he and his warriors would turn on the British and cut them to pieces if Proctor retreated. His threat was taken seriously; Tecumseh's warriors outnumbered the British regulars three to one.

On September 18, Elliot brokered a meeting between Tecumseh, Proctor, and the military advisors. Tecumseh accused the British of breaking their promise and abandoning his people. He reminded the assembly that they had not yet seen an American soldier in Amherstburg, and that they had yet to be defeated on Canadian soil. Proctor then made his case for retreat. The British would, he promised, meet the enemy at a more strategic location along the Thames Valley, just 60 kilometres to the northeast. This would draw the Americans toward the east, deeper into Canadian territory and farther from reinforcements and supplies.

Tecumseh called Proctor a "miserable old squaw,"[5] and accused the British of being "a fat dog that carries its tail on its back but when affrighted, drops it between its legs and runs off."[6] But his words did not persuade. The decision to retreat had been made. Tecumseh was trapped in his alliance with Proctor; he had no choice but to follow the retreat. With great misgivings, he told his warriors, "We are going to follow the British, but I fear I will never return."[7]

Proctor led the retreat. Within a few days, the British had abandoned all of the Michigan territory captured by Brock the previous year. Appalled by the lack of definitive action, and believing the British to be facing defeat, half of Tecumseh's warriors deserted during the retreat. Finally, Proctor halted the retreat at a Native village called Moraviantown. Tecumseh and the warriors scouted

Map of the Battle of the Thames.

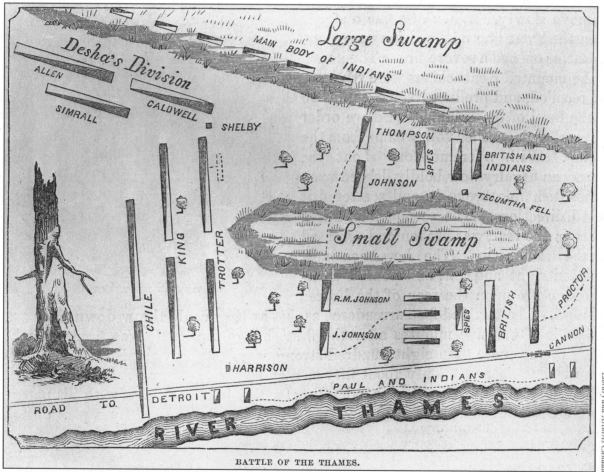

BATTLE OF THE THAMES.

Library and Archives Canada

behind the troops and acted as a rearguard. In an effort to delay the advance of the Americans, Tecumseh stopped a few kilometres south of the village to destroy a bridge and skirmish with American scouts. But this did not slow Harrison's troops for long.

That evening, Tecumseh stopped at a mill while he waited for some of his warriors to catch up to him. The settler who owned the mill, Christopher Arnold, was terrified. A band of Native warriors had burned his neighbour's mill a few days before, and he thought he was in for the same treatment. Tecumseh knew that his warriors had been told to burn everything that might be of use to the Americans. But he also realized the settlers were low on food and depended on the mill. He stayed the night to protect the mill from his own men.

The next morning, October 5, 1813, Tecumseh asked Arnold to watch for American scouts while he waited in the woods, ready to gallop off to warn the British at the first sign of them. He told the miller to pretend he was digging and to throw up a shovel of earth as soon as he saw the scouts. Arnold readily agreed. However, Tecumseh's sharp eyes found the scouts first and he was gone before Arnold had a chance to give him the signal. On his way to join Proctor, Tecumseh performed another act of charity. Arnold had told him that his brother-in-law's family had no food. The miller had wanted to take them some flour, but was afraid to venture out. So, on his way to join the troops, Tecumseh rode by the brother-in-law's house and tossed a bag of flour at the front door.

Tecumseh reached the troops and began to prepare for combat. He was still eager to fight, but had misgivings about the looming battle. Proctor had not discussed strategy with him. The troops had not eaten in days, they were low on ammunition, and they were greatly outnumbered. Proctor had barely 500 regulars and militiamen and by then Tecumseh commanded only 500 warriors. Harrison was fast approaching with more than 3,000 well-armed men. Tecumseh directed the battle strategy. He positioned his warriors on the far edge of a great swamp, and placed Proctor and his men to the left on some high ground between the Thames River and the swamp. He told the militia to take up a position between the two groups.

Reviewing the position of the British, Tecumseh cautioned Proctor to stand firm. Then he returned to the swamp to wait. No trace of the compassionate, literate man remained. With war paint on his face, and hate in his eyes, Tecumseh was the quintessential warrior. The American troops arrived at the battleground and the two armies faced each other for several hours, barely 275 metres apart, while the Americans formed their lines. Finally, they were ready for combat. One battalion charged the British, then a group of Kentucky militiamen advanced toward Tecumseh. The hardened men yelled, "Remember River Raisin," as they spurred their horses forward. As Tecumseh had predicted, the horses got bogged down in the thick marsh, and the Americans were forced to continue on foot. Tecumseh's warriors quickly cut them down.

This respite did not last long. Along the high ground, the British line had broken and Proctor's soldiers were running for their lives. Tecumseh and his men had been abandoned. Harrison's troops closed in on the warriors. When the warriors ran out of ammunition, they fought on with their tomahawks. Tecumseh's chilling war cry echoed through the forest, then, suddenly, it was silenced.

Words Tecumseh had spoken just a few days earlier might have still been on his mind as he fell. "Our lives are in the hands of the Great Spirit. We are determined to defend our lands, and if it is His will, we wish to leave our bones upon them."[8]

The great chief was never found. It is generally believed that the warriors took his body with them when they retreated. There is no official record of Tecumseh's death and no official marker over his final resting place. But, to this day, the Shawnee elders say they know where he is buried and that the location of his grave has been passed down from one generation of select leaders to the next.

Wherever Tecumseh lies, the hopes of a Native peoples' confederacy are buried with him. The grand alliance between the Native peoples and the British was finished. The last of the nations made peace with the Americans, and the lands that Tecumseh had fought to keep free were sold to settlers. The Native peoples of Tecumseh's generation lived the rest of their lives on small parcels of reserved lands. "The great barrier was broken," wrote one of his followers. "It was my last fight. My heart was big then, Tecumseh filled it. It has been empty ever since."[9]

The Death of Tecumseh.

After the Battle of the Thames, Proctor was court-martialled for negligence and incompetence. Suspended from his post, he lived out the rest of his days in disgrace. Brigadier General Harrison, lacking adequate supplies for the coming winter, was unable to capitalize on his victory. He soon retreated back to Fort Detroit.

The war was at a stalemate once more, and the borders were much the same as they had been in the early months of the war.

TECUMSEH

CHAPTER SIX:
RED GEORGE AND THE HIGHLANDERS

George Richard John Macdonnell was that interesting hybrid of early 19th century Canadian, neither entirely Canadian nor completely British. "Red George," as he was called to distinguish him from the numerous other Macdonnells in Upper Canada, was a born military man with a deep pride, a fiery temper, and an abundance of confidence. He was born in Newfoundland to the wife of the commander of Fort Townshend, John Macdonnell. The elder Macdonnell had been a hero of Culloden. And like his clansman John Macdonnell, Brock's right-hand man, George Macdonnell would prove to be one of Canada's most valuable heroes. After a brief stint serving in Europe, persistent rumours of an impending invasion by the United States brought Red George back to Canada.

While Red George was preparing to return to defend the country of his birth, a group of his clansmen were also preparing for war. By 1804, the Scottish Highlands were facing dire economic times and a recently disbanded group of ex-soldiers of the Glengarry Clan had suffered more than most. Led by their priest, Alexander Macdonell, they immigrated to Glengarry County, Upper Canada, to join other clansmen who had had moved into the area from New York State as United Empire Loyalists. They quickly adopted their new country as their own and were fierce in their defence of it. These were a different group of settlers, bred in the craggy Highlands and hardened by their service in the Seven Years War. When the whispers of an impending war with the United States grew louder, these Scots, like so many other Canadians, became convinced that the various insults offered by the Americans were merely an excuse for the annexation of Canada.

The Glengarry Macdonells sent a delegation to Governor General George Prevost asking that their old regiment be resurrected so they could assist in the protection of Canada. Unsurprisingly, Prevost agreed. He immediately sent for their clansman Red George, who was then serving as a captain with the 8th Regiment in Nova Scotia, and assigned him to act as a recruiting agent for the new force. They would be called the Glengarry Light Infantry Fencibles. The regiment, like the Macdonells, was devoutly Roman Catholic and the priest who had originally brought them to Canada — Alexander Macdonell — would become the first Roman Catholic chaplain in the British Army in hundreds of years. Alexander Macdonell would later become a bishop and one of the highest ranking Roman Catholic priests in Upper Canada. Red George recognized a perfect opportunity to advance his career and wholeheartedly embraced his job as recruiter. He was quickly promoted for his recruiting efforts, eventually retaining the rank of lieutenant-colonel. Eventually he would be given command of all the troops stationed at Fort Wellington.

The Fencibles were initially sent to help guard the small village of Prescott. At that time, Prescott was a vital link in the supply chain for the British Army. Ships coming from Great Britain would sail to Montreal where the goods they carried would be transferred onto smaller, flat-bottomed bateaux for the perilous journey over the rapids that stretched between Montreal and Prescott. From Prescott they sailed to Kingston where the goods were transferred onto larger ships before proceeding on their journey to York or one of the forts along the Niagara. It was a dangerous journey that was made even more dangerous by the U.S. declaration of war in August 1812. The war seemed even more real to the Fencibles at Prescott. The rapids measured a mere mile across at the town and on the other side sat the enemy, in the form of the American village of Ogdensburg. While they cleared the top of the rapids at Prescott, the precious supplies destined for the British Army were at their most vulnerable, an easy mark for the Americans. Red George had another worry: if the Americans decided to take the lightly defended Prescott they could easily create a stranglehold on supplies that would destroy the British.

For most of 1812, the British commanders were too occupied with the western battlefields to give much thought to their supply chain to the east. It fell to the local militia — the Glengarry Fencibles — to make what rudimentary defences

Windmill Point, near Prescott.

they could at Prescott. They began with two buildings along the river and erected a wooden stockade around them. Then they built another for defence closer to the river and mounted two nine-pound guns on it. But no one believed that could keep out the Americans for long if they decided to attack the town.

By December 1812, the war had spread into Lake Ontario and Prevost ordered the construction of a large one-storey blockhouse and a series of ramparts christened Fort Wellington. But in keeping with his belief that his role was primarily that of defender, Prevost forbade any attacks on the Americans. Eager to test his mettle and that of his new regiment, Macdonnell chafed at Prevost's orders but he obeyed.

For the first year of the war, the town fathers of Ogdensburg had managed to fend off any attempts to house a garrison there and matters between the two villages went on almost as they always had. In fact, trade between the two flourished as the war created shortages and prices spiked. Smuggling was always a highly profitable and common industry in border towns and the war merely served to expand it. In early 1812, Ogdensburg farmer David Parish marched his herd of cattle across the frozen St. Lawrence River to earn a profit three times what he

Smuggling

If smuggling was a thriving enterprise before the War of 1812, it exploded during the war. Efforts by the Americans to restrict trade with Canadians and British merely attracted additional legitimate traders to the more profitable practice of smuggling. With a large army to maintain, the British were willing to pay high prices and, unlike the Americans, paid in gold.

The smugglers used specially constructed roads and trails in the summer and in the winter they hauled their goods across the frozen lakes and rivers, braving increasingly hefty fines imposed by their own government. Banks in both Boston and Philadelphia were openly willing to fund smuggling enterprises and British trading licences became hot commodities on the open market. Beef and other foodstuffs, timber, and war supplies were delivered to the eager British via hollowed-out sleighs, false-bottomed boxes, and even coffins, while American officials were bribed to look the other way.

Even the most active theatres of war were not immune to smuggling. David Parrish of Ogdensburg marched his cattle right across the frozen St. Lawrence River in order to receive three times as much money as he would have received from his fellow Americans. And while the British blockaded Chesapeake Bay, they lived on rations cheerfully supplied by the industrious citizens of the area. At one point in the war, the British General Prevost remarked that two-thirds of his soldiers were surviving on enemy beef. This stood in stark contrast to the American troops serving in isolated northern posts, who were frequently short of food and supplies.

CANADA ON FIRE

might expect at home, while his neighbours marvelled as nearly 1,000 sleigh-loads of provisions made their way past his house on their way to Prescott. This trade became so important to the war effort that at one point Prevost estimated that two thirds of the troops under his command were living on enemy beef. There were, of course, courts set up to prosecute smugglers but town leaders and the militia, many of whom were farmers and businessmen themselves, frequently turned a blind eye and might have unwittingly kept the British war machine alive.

While the relationship between the townsfolk on both sides of the rapids was friendly, it was only a matter of time before the reality of war came to Prescott and Ogdensburg. In early 1813, it finally arrived in the person of Captain John Forsythe, the commander of an American Rifle Regiment. Captain Forsythe had been given the task of protecting the good people of Ogdensburg and of keeping watch for any movement on the part of the British. Like Macdonnell, Forsythe was also reluctantly obeying orders not to launch any attacks against the enemy. He was to wait and watch and he did, watching primarily for an excuse to cross the river. He did not have to wait long. On February 4, he learned that members of the American militia were being held in the jails at Elizabethtown and there was a possibility that they were being mistreated. Two days later, an outraged Forsythe mustered his men and marched them 45 kilometres to Elizabethtown, sleighs in tow to accommodate any booty they might find. At 3:00 a.m. they surrounded the jail. The Elizabethtown militia was still fast asleep. They quickly gave up the keys to the jail. The only opposition the Rifles faced was a solitary shot fired from a nearby window, perhaps by a jittery citizen. Forsythe quickly commanded that the prisoners be freed except for one man who stood accused of murder. Then, scooping up several prominent men as hostages, he and his men retreated back across the river.

Macdonnell was furious when he heard of Forsythe's actions and demanded that Prevost allow him to retaliate. But Prevost, ever cautious, ordered him to stand down and not engage the Americans. His position, Prevost claimed, was to remain defensive. But along the St. Lawrence River the citizens were growing more nervous. If Forsythe could slip into Elizabethtown completely unopposed were any of them truly safe? Bolstered by his success at Elizabethtown, and the obvious reluctance of the Canadians and British to retaliate, Forsythe continued to cross the river. As the weeks went by, he grew bolder, his raids more frequent. The British command viewed him as a nuisance, a thief who plundered and raided. But to Macdonnell he was a constant irritation, like salt poured over and over again into a wound that refused to heal.

In mid-February, Macdonnell learned that Forsythe's men had slipped across the ice and stolen horses from a farmer near Prescott. Outraged, he sent men to Ogdensburg to demand their immediate return. Forsythe denied knowing anything about the horses and then offered Macdonnell a greater insult. He ordered Macdonnell's men back to Fort Wellington and then loudly announced that he'd gladly meet their commander, "Red George," on the ice at the next available opportunity. The challenge had been issued and Macdonnell was all too happy to meet it.

When Prevost visited Fort Wellington a few days later, Macdonnell relayed the tales of Forsythe's activities and again urged the governor general to give him permission to attack. When Prevost again demurred, Macdonnell offered more incentive. Forsythe, he suggested, knew by now of the governor's presence at Fort Wellington. Prevost was quite obviously in grave danger. What a feather in his cap it would be for Forsythe to capture the king's representative. Prevost was frightened and commandeered a large portion of Fort Wellington's soldiers to guard him on his way to Kingston, but he told Macdonnell to stay put. However, Prevost did allow Macdonnell and his men to practise manoeuvres on the ice to help distract and discourage the enemy from attacking Prevost and his entourage.

This was all the encouragement that Macdonnell needed. He thrived on combat and this time the grudge was a personal one. He was going to end Forsythe's raids once and for all. The American raider had holed up less than a mile away at Ogdensburg and Macdonnell could almost see him mocking the British and Canadians from the safety of his fort. Within hours, Macdonnell had mustered just over 100 regulars and over 400 militia, and ordered the regiment's field guns mounted on sleighs. Macdonnell ordered one third of his men to head straight across the river with the guns while he led the rest farther downriver to subdue the village of Ogdensburg and then attack Forsythe's flank. As he paused to breakfast at Elizabethtown, the ever-cautious Prevost, perhaps suspecting the volatile personality of his commander, had sent yet another message to Macdonnell ordering him to stand down. But Macdonnell had already left the fort. A bitter February wind whipped down the St. Lawrence, forming drifts more impenetrable than the most formidable battery. Loud cracks rent the air like gunshots beneath the feet of the men and the sleighs as they struggled across the ice, but they continued toward their target.

The Americans were used to seeing the Canadians drilling out on the ice, so at first they ignored the gathering of men that appeared to be heading toward their shore. When the Canadian bugler called the charge on the fort, the Americans were stunned. Within the fort, Forsythe finally ordered his Riflers toward the walls. They immediately turned the fort's big guns on the columns of men marching toward them on the ice. The first ferocious volley turned over the Canadian cannon and killed the only Canadian gunners who knew how to use it. The British and Canadians were easy targets, lined up like sitting ducks as they moved slowly across the ice. When they reached the drifts closer to shore, the Canadians' big guns became stuck, rendered useless against Forsythe's defence. The Canadian and British soldiers were forced to wade through waist-deep snow to get closer to the fort. Once they cleared the drifts they were within range of Forsythe's riflemen and completely exposed. At the head of the force was an unlikely sight, Alexander Macdonell, the chaplain, holding a cross high above his head as he trudged forward, and at his side a Presbyterian minister holding a Bible above his head. They appeared oblivious to the explosions of the big guns and the rain of grapeshot that was decimating the column all around them. When the chaplain noticed a nervous man sinking back to the relative safety of the rear of the column, he ordered the man to keep going. When the man refused, the furious chaplain excommunicated him on the spot. A witness later reported that it would have been better for the hapless soldier to have faced the enemy than the wrath of Alexander Macdonell, for "when the enemy being in front, his blood was up and the terrors of the Church were at his disposal."[1]

Also leading the attack was a Captain Jenkins. As he led the charge toward the beach, Jenkins was felled by a volley of grapeshot that shattered his arm. Seeing his men falter, he forced himself to his feet and shouted to them to "never mind me." Jenkins continued to lead the men closer to the fort until he was felled again — this time for good — by another volley. On the snowy beach a wounded private by the name of Thomas Ross sank down against a log. Despite his wounds, Ross propped himself against the log and continued to fire at the enemy until an enemy musket ball finally shattered his weapon. Despite the heroic efforts of so many men like Jenkins and Ross, the frontal attack was in disarray. With heavy losses and their captain critically wounded, they soon abandoned the attack and moved downstream toward Macdonnell.

The main force under Macdonnell was having a much easier time in the lightly defended village. Virtually unopposed, they swept through the village until, on a desolate street, they came face to face with a cannon manned by Captain Giles Kellogg and his company. Unfortunately for Kellogg, he had expected the attack to come from a different direction and valuable time was wasted while his men turned the cannon around to face the enemy. As the Canadians marched forward, the Americans were appalled to discover that in their haste they had broken the screw that was used to elevate the cannon. They hastily abandoned their position and withdrew to the fort, leaving the local sheriff, a man named York, to fend off the Canadians as best he could. With a tiny six-pounder, the Sheriff and his men valiantly fired at the advancing Canadians until they were forced to flee for their lives. Only York remained. The Canadians approached with their muskets while the Sheriff continued to fire at them. Admiring the man's bravery, Red George ordered them to stand down, claiming that York was too brave a man to kill.

Once the village was captured, "Red George" turned his attention to the fort and the decimated remains of his original frontal force. With his fort surrounded, Forsythe ordered it abandoned. The Americans retreated, leaving both the town and the fort in the hands of the Canadians and British. In his rush to flee, Forsythe left behind his sword, which was seized by the Canadian militia and still hangs as a trophy in Fort Wellington. Macdonnell's men worked quickly to secure the American's artillery, ordnance, and supplies and began the slow process of transporting them back across the frozen, slippery river. Seventy prisoners also accompanied the loot. The Highlanders were unable to remove the two armed schooners moored in the harbour, the *Niagara* and the *Dolphin*, because they were mired in thick ice, so they burned them along with the barracks and several smaller boats. Inflamed by the ferocity of battle, and perhaps angered by the deaths of so many from Jenkins's main force, the men turned their attention to the rich stores of the town.

But Macdonnell was determined to protect the honour of his regiment. He forbade any looting and placed sentries about the town to enforce his orders. Several stories are told about his protection of prisoners who were receiving harsh treatment by their captors, insisting that all be treated with respect. When Ogdensburg's wagons and wagoneers were conscripted to assist in transporting the weapons and stores to Prescott, Macdonnell offered to pay them four dollars per day in hard silver for their efforts. Reportedly, no one refused the offer. Macdonnell's revenge stood in stark contrast to Forsythe's actions and it did not go unappreciated by the people of Ogdensburg. Once Macdonnell had gone back to Prescott, they sent a delegation to Washington requesting that no more garrisons be stationed at Ogdensburg. Their request was granted and Ogdensburg, unlike so many other border towns, was able to maintain at least an appearance of neutrality. For the remaining months of the war, the village would serve as a major, albeit surreptitious, source of supplies for the British Army and Canadian militia.

Given the success of the raid, Prevost had no choice but to praise it. And in an increasingly typical display of credit-taking where none was due, he even altered Macdonnell's official report of the raid so that it would appear that he had given Macdonnell orders to attack. Macdonnell was slightly injured in the attack and spent much of the spring of 1813 recovering. The many visitors during his recovery included some of the citizens of Ogdensburg. Once he had recovered, Macdonnell was given command of the 1st Light Infantry battalion, an ad hoc mélange of volunteers and conscripts selected by a lottery to serve for one year.

In the fall of 1813, the Americans launched most of their largest and most complex assaults on Canada. American Generals Wilkinson and Hampton launched a two-pronged attack with the objective of taking Montreal. Charles-Michel de Salaberry and his Voltigeurs were sent out to intercept Hampton, but while they were as fearless as Macdonnell's Highlanders they were also desperately outmanned and in obvious need of reinforcement. Macdonnell was still in the midst of training his new battalion, most of whom still lacked a proper uniform. He had just sat down to a late dinner when an agitated Prevost rode up to ask how quickly Macdonnell could ready his troops. "As soon as they finish their dinner," the unflappable Macdonnell was said to have replied.

Macdonnell faced a seemingly insurmountable problem. There was no time for an overland march. They had to get to de Salaberry as quickly as possible. The infamous St. Lawrence rapids provided the quickest route, but also the most perilous. An undaunted Macdonnell procured the necessary boats and, lacking sailors to man them, he set his soldiers to oar while he served as pilot. They survived the rapids intact and then made their way along the St. Lawrence River in their motley collection of boats while a wicked storm raged around them. Arriving at the shore in the dead of night, they began a trek through the woods in single file before finally arriving at the bank of the Châteauguay River. They had made the trek from Kingston to the Châteauguay — a distance of over 310 kilometres — in less than 60 hours, narrowly missing a confrontation with the American Major-General James Wilkinson's force on Lake Ontario. Prevost arrived soon after, having used a series of relay horses to race along the bank of the St. Lawrence River. Seeing Macdonnell, a stunned Prevost demanded to know where his men were. Macdonnell pointed to a section of the ground, littered with exhausted soldiers. "There," he replied. All 600 men had made the trip and were now resting while they awaited their orders.

Using a combination of bravado and unorthodox tactics, Macdonnell and the 1st battalion would play a decisive role in repelling the American attack at Châteauguay. Following the battle, Macdonnell also participated in a number of skirmishes and was given the task of inspecting and training the numerous companies of Canadian militia scattered over Upper and Lower Canada. As a result, he was a familiar sight in forts like Fort York, Fort George, Kingston, and Cornwall. In his role as inspector, Macdonnell realized how vulnerable the single supply line along the St. Lawrence made Canada. He explored an alternate route along the Rideau River and developed a rudimentary plan for a canal with temporary dams and crude wooden structures. He claimed that Prevost had offered him 2,000 guineas if he could draft a workable plan for an alternate route but he was denied the reward because the Colonial Office declared the existence of a similar set of plans drafted much earlier than Macdonnell's.

In 1816, Macdonnell returned to England to marry a prominent member of Scottish society. Despite the commendations he received for Châteauguay, he became increasingly bitter at what he felt was a lack of appreciation for his numerous sacrifices in the defence of Canada. His claims grew more preposterous as he aged and little recognition was forthcoming. Brock's tactics at the beginning of the war were, he claimed, entirely inspired by him and his victory at Ogdensburg was of "one hundred times more importance" than Nelson's victory at Trafalgar. Macdonnell had, he claimed, saved the English empire. For many, Macdonnell's military brilliance was dimmed by his ridiculous claims. But his victories in Canada helped change the course of the war and helped ensure a Canadian victory.

CHAPTER SEVEN:
JOHN STRACHAN AND
THE DEFENCE OF YORK

Like Brock, Dr. John Strachan was a reluctant immigrant to Canada. And also like Brock, he became one of the fledgling colony's most ardent defenders. Strachan was born in 1778 in Aberdeen to a Scottish quarry worker and his wife. His father's sudden death in a mine explosion rendered the humble family destitute and as the eldest of the nine Strachan children, John was forced to go to work to support his mother and siblings. His experiences would make him a strong man but not an especially tolerant one — especially of failure or weakness — a personality trait that would define his experiences during the War of 1812.

Strachan took work as a tutor and still managed to complete his divinity degree from King's College. In 1799, faced with the realities of supporting his mother and sisters, Strachan was forced to abandon his dream of teaching at one of the universities and accept a job offer from the governor of Upper Canada, John Graves Simcoe, who commissioned Strachan to overhaul the education system in Canada. After an exceedingly long and stormy voyage across the Atlantic, Strachan arrived to find that Simcoe had resigned and his position was in limbo. "If I had had twenty pounds in my pocket," he said afterward to a friend, "I should have returned to Scotland immediately. But in truth I had not so much as twenty shillings. So I had to stay."[1]

In Canada, Strachan made his living as a minister and eventually helped found a grammar school in present-day Cornwall, Ontario. There he taught some of colony's best and brightest, including a young John Beverley Robinson who would eventually become lieutenant governor of Ontario. But as rumblings of war reached a crescendo on the other side of Lake Ontario, Strachan accepted a new position in the provincial capital of York, a move that would bring him right into the centre of the war. He, his wife, and daughters loaded their possessions onto a shallow bateau and ponderously made their way down the St. Lawrence River and then across the length of Lake Ontario from Cornwall to the provincial capital of York. The journey, a long and arduous one in the best of circumstances, was rendered even more precarious when the United States declared war on Britain just as the Strachan family boarded a schooner to cross Lake Ontario.

As they crossed the lake, all eyes were on the horizon. A strange ship in the distance paralyzed the captain, who feared they were about to be boarded by invading Americans. Strachan was forced to take charge, ordering the schooner's single gun to be made ready. The ship turned out to be Canadian, no shots were exchanged, and the Strachans safely landed at York. The provincial capital must have been a bit of disappointment to the Strachans after their experiences in the relative sophistication of Cornwall. In 1812, York was a tiny, poorly defended village with a population that barely topped 600. Most of its buildings were rough and made of wood — either log homes or framed one-storey structures. Only two were made of brick. Many of the structures had earth floors, though some had floors made of wood, and the roadways were little more than rough dirt paths. Even the houses of parliament were little more than a collection of humble wooden buildings amusingly dubbed the Palaces of Parliament. Although there was some movement to establish York as a major shipbuilding interest, in 1812 its importance to Upper Canada was still far more symbolic than strategic.

The winter of 1812–13 produced an excess of bad news for the Americans. At best, the invasion of Canada that was expected to be a "mere matter of marching" was at a stalemate. The American defeat at Queenston Heights was followed by a few lacklustre successes and many more significant failures, like those at River Raisin, Frenchtown, and Ogdensburg. To make matters worse, the British had set up a naval blockade that extended most of the way down the U.S. east coast, ensuring easy access to both supplies and reinforcements. If they wanted any hope of victory, the Americans would have to cut off the British supply line to Upper Canada. As Brock had warned in the early days of the war, the fate of Canada lay in who had naval control of Lakes Erie and Ontario.

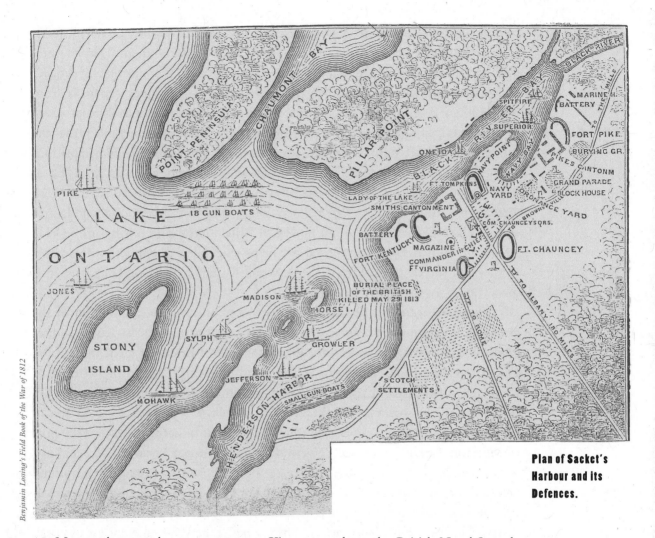

Benjamin Lossing's Field Book of the War of 1812

Montreal was a clear target, as was Kingston, where the British Naval Squadron was based. Believing Montreal to be the more problematic target, United States Secretary of War John Armstrong ordered Senior Major-General Henry Dearborn to cross the frozen St. Lawrence River and attack Kingston. In February, word reached Dearborn that Governor-General Sir George Prevost was en route to Kingston and that the city's garrison had grown to over 6,000 men. He believed an attack on the American garrison at Sackets Harbor was imminent. Despite intelligence that reported the actual numbers at Kingston to be considerably smaller — less than 600 regulars and 1,400 militia — and Prevost's quick departure from the fort, Dearborn remained convinced that Kingston was beyond his reach.

Instead, Dearborn argued for an invasion of the far more vulnerable provincial capital of York. He pointed to the possibility of capturing two key acquisitions of the British Navy: the *Sir Isaac Brock*, under construction in the dockyard at York, and the *Prince Regent*, a warship wintering in the provincial capital. Both were important prizes. The *Brock*, when completed, would be the second largest ship on Lake Ontario and would be key to British naval superiority on the lake. American politicians were intrigued by the propaganda value inherent in an easy victory and the capture of the enemy capital. By early spring of 1813, they had given Dearborn his orders to attack.

A force consisting of 12 schooners, associated officers, and marines under the command of Commodore Isaac Chauncey gathered alongside the 1,600 soldiers who would form the invasion force under the lead of Brigadier General Zebulon Pike. Command of the entire force was ceded to Henry Dearborn. It would be the first United States Army-Navy combined amphibious assault in history. On April 23, a strong storm forced the American flotilla to turn back. Under cover of that same storm, the *Prince Regent* quietly sailed out of harm's way into the port of Kingston. Isaac Brock's replacement, General Sir Roger Sheaffe, had been urging his superiors to put York into a more respectable state of defence[2] but nothing was done. As the American fleet set sail on April 24, Sheaffe ordered government officials to hide official documents in the forests behind the town and ordered the town itself to stand ready for attack. Sheaffe had a mere 700 men at his disposal, including about 50 Mississauga and Ojibwa warriors, assorted dockworkers and navy personnel, and 350 mostly inexperienced militia. In the months prior to the invasion, the government had started the highly questionable practice of pulling regulars from York and replacing them with militiamen who, after a few weeks of training, were cycled out to other forts and replaced with new recruits from the countryside. While the locals praised the patriotism and enthusiasm of the new recruits, it would soon become clear that neither was a substitute for experience.

In sharp contrast to the storms that had buffeted the shores earlier in the week, the evening of April 26th was calm and clear. High above the lake, on the Scarborough Bluffs, a sentry logged an extraordinary account of what he saw that night as the setting sun cast fading golden rays over the water: a scene of tranquility and beauty that would stand in sharp contrast to the chaos and bloodshed that were about to occur. As the tall ships sailed toward York, the sentry noted the enchanting spectacle they made on the lake, their snow-white canvases billowing in the wind. It proved to the calm before the storm. Suddenly the boom of a signal gun rent the air, warning York of the impending invasion. Again and again it sounded, almost immediately echoed by the incessant pealing of the bells of St. James Cathedral calling the militiamen to arms. The American schooners came to rest just offshore of the site of the old French Fort of Toronto, about two kilometres west of York. Their silence in the gathering twilight was probably more ominous than the sound of the signal gun. As darkness fell, everyone settled in for an uneasy night of waiting.

Dawn brought no relief as the American ships continued to wait offshore in silent menace. Sheaffe, the regulars, and militia gathered in the fort. The few ancient guns available to the defenders received a small complement of men while numerous other more modern guns, destined for the decks of the still unfinished *Sir Isaac Brock*, lay untouched beneath the snow and mud. Before the American ships arrived, John Strachan had already sent his wife and daughters to what he believed to be the safe haven of Cornwall. At 4:00 on the morning of August 27 he woke and immediately mounted his horse to ride the garrison. He would later write to a friend that he was unafraid but feared the commander (Sheaffe) was too weak. Around 8:00 a.m., gazing through a spy glass, Strachan saw the decks of the American ships "crowded with men."[3]

While Strachan questioned why no troops were sent to prevent the Americans from landing, Sheaffe did launch a somewhat half-hearted, piecemeal attempt to repel the attack. But the men were deployed in small, isolated groups over a wide area, and none stood any chance of stopping the Americans. The first group to be sent out were the Mississauga and Ojibwa, under the command of Major James Givins of the Indian Department. The Glengarry Infantry was next, followed by a small contingent of militiamen sent to guard the road. After further delays, additional groups were sent one at a time toward the landing area. With the Glengarry Infantry lost in the woods, and a later group electing to join the troops on the road rather than proceed to the landing area, the Americans quickly overcame the Natives and began their march on the town. A last ditch attempt by the Grenadiers forced some of the Americans back to their boats, but dozens of people were killed in the battle that followed. With their overwhelming numbers, the Americans soon rallied and the Grenadiers were forced to flee the beach and take refuge in the woods. More pitched battles were fought before a beleaguered Sheaffe finally decided to call a retreat.

The motley crew of retreating soldiers made their way to a gunnery known as the Western Battery. Protected by an earthen mound, they watched as the two groups of gunners fired a pair of decommissioned 18-pounders that had been hastily repaired, propped up, and secured to wooden stocks. But they had barely found that refuge when the magazine suddenly exploded. The guns were blown off their makeshift mounts and over a dozen men were killed. But it was the wounded that shocked most observers. With blackened faces, scorched clothes, and horrific burns, they were carried away toward the garrison by whatever means could be found. One militiaman recounted the horrifying site of a soldier, who appeared to have broken all of his bones in the blast, being carried from the site in a wheelbarrow. Not willing to give up, two of the militia stayed behind as their fellow soldiers were evacuated. They hurriedly retrieved one of the 18-pounders and struggled to get it set up again, only to find that there was no grapeshot left. They too were forced to continue the retreat back to the garrison.

The retreating troops reached the garrison around noon, with the Americans close behind. The garrison offered little protection. The minimal earthworks that surrounded it barely gave the Americans pause and the handful of guns it contained offered little resistance. Within the hour, Sheaffe had decided to abandon the fort, taking all that was left of his regular soldiers with him and leaving the militia and villagers to negotiate whatever terms they could. A bewildered Strachan, like the Americans, was still waiting for Sheaffe to launch a counterattack. Seeing the retreat, Strachan asked several of the officers what was happening. He was stunned to be told that "they had no orders, there is no plan of attack … no future point of resistance mentioned."[4] Disgusted, Strachan returned to the hospital to treat the wounded. But as he was arriving there, a sudden explosion rocked the town and a huge plume of smoke appeared above the magazine.

What Strachan did not know was that Sheaffe had ordered a fuse lit on the garrison's magazine. The explosion blew the magazine to pieces and a hail of masonry and wooden beams rained down on American, British, and Canadian soldiers. Just beneath the magazine, the American General Pike had paused beneath a tree to interrogate a captured British soldier. Like scores of his men, Pike was fatally wounded in the explosion. The explosion dramatically increased the cost of the victory for the Americans who had suffered comparatively few casualties during the battle itself. When the numbers were finally counted, the Americans had 72 killed and 220 wounded compared to the British and Canadians, who had lost 62 men with another 94 wounded. The Americans believed that the British had exploded an underground mine and while their general was evacuated back to the ships, they awaited what they believed would be an imminent attack from the British. The attack failed to materialize and with the British flag still flying high above the garrison, the Americans were not sure what to expect.

Faced with continuing silence from the garrison, the Americans finally sent a contingent under a flag of truce. They were met by two militia leaders and Strachan, all of whom were anxious to negotiate terms that would protect the town and the remaining militiamen. It was two in the afternoon and a great huzzah was heard as the British flag was brought down and the American flag hoisted above the provincial capital. One of the American soldiers took a corner of the British flag to the ship where General Pike lay dying, and tucked it under his pillow. In less than six hours, the battle was over. The Americans had still seen no sign of Sheaffe, who was already well on his way to the safety of Kingston, racing far ahead of his men on his horse. The Americans were not pleased to be negotiating with the militia and at first they refused to even discuss terms. As another plume of smoke rose to the west, the negotiations broke down completely. As he raced out of town, Sheaffe had set fire to the shipyards, destroying the American's most valued prize — the *Sir Isaac Brock*. Talks were abruptly adjourned and because an entire day went by without signed terms, the Canadians were unable to parole

Field Hospitals

"Wading in blood, I cut and slashed for forty-eight hours without food or sleep."

The American surgeon Dr. William Beaumont described his work in the hours following the explosions at York in April 1813, in letters to his family. The horrors of the battlefields were often echoed in the field hospitals set up just beyond the reach of musket fire. They were dark, dirty, depressing places but they offered the only chance of survival for the wounded — if the soldiers ever got there. The wounded would lie for hours, occasionally days, before they could be safely transported to these temporary infirmaries. The ride there was rough, often on makeshift stretchers fashioned from bayonets and greatcoats or via wooden carts pulled by oxen or the surviving soldiers.

Once he reached the field hospital, little relief awaited the wounded soldier. Amputation was the most common treatment for broken bones and deep wounds. Anaesthetics didn't exist. Instead, the soldier would be given a draught of whisky and a strap of leather to bite down on while his mates held him down and the surgeon worked the saw. Even with amputation, infection was common and its most common treatment was bloodletting, generally to the point where the patient lost consciousness.

Wounds were not the only problem the doctors had to deal with. Crowded, frequently unsanitary conditions, and men already weakened by the weeks of battle and hard living conditions proved to be excellent breeding grounds for disease. In fact, many more soldiers would die of disease than would die of their wounds. Yet the men, like Dr. William "Tiger" Dunlop and Dr. William Beaumont, worked tirelessly and drastically reduced the casualty rates during the war.

their wounded. Prisoners and the wounded and dying were detained at the garrison, denied treatment or even basic sustenance.

They lay there for 48 hours until, after some heated exchanges, Strachan was finally able to force the Americans to provide at least a meal to the prisoners, but they were not given medical treatment. Strachan was also increasingly worried about the safety of the townspeople. The riflemen who had been assigned to protect the town had been actively involved in looting it. A few of the more honourable Americans intervened and tried to protect the townsfolk, but it was clear that the majority of the Americans were restless after their time aboard ship, the relatively brief exertions of battle, and their failure to secure the prizes they sought. Most were intent on taking out their frustrations on the town. More often than not, attempts to intervene were met with the barrel of a musket. The local sheriff, John Beikie, was also helpless and, like Strachan, he bitterly complained of Sheaffe's cowardly abandonment of the town. "He left us," Beikie wrote, "standing in the street like a parcel of sheep."[5] Strachan is much more harsh in his condemnation of Sheaffe, saying that he was "destitute of the military fire and vigour of decision which the principal commander in this country must possess in order to preserve it."[6] Whatever strategic or military purposes that might have been served by Sheaffe's hurried retreat were lost in the universal condemnation of his actions in leaving the people of York at the mercy of the marauding American Army. Strachan's star continued to rise and it was largely due to his influence that Governor General Prevost replaced Sheaffe as commander. Sheaffe's career in Canada would never recover and he was soon recalled to Britain.

In the meantime, a frustrated Strachan demanded an interview with Henry Dearborn, who had refused to leave the relative comfort of his ship. When Dearborn did finally go ashore the next morning he was in no mood to negotiate. Furious that over 250 of his men, including General Pike, had died in what he believed to be an explosion set by a dishonourable Canadian militia, he entered the garrison vowing that the town would burn. Undeterred, Strachan pointed out that the militia lost men in the explosion as well and it was highly unlikely they would have set a charge that would kill their own men. Eventually, Dearborn was appeased, and he finally agreed to that the town and its people would go unmolested. The militia would be paroled, meaning they could return to their homes if they agreed not to fight again until an "exchange" could be made with American prisoners.

The wounded militia and regimentals were taken to a makeshift hospital. Unfortunately, Sheaffe had taken all of the regimental surgeons with him, leaving only a handful of local medics to care for the wounded. To make matters worse, the official truce had no effect on the American soldiers. The looting continued unabated. To many it seemed to worsen. People who resisted were threatened. On April 30th, Strachan's church was set ablaze and a few hours later the legislature was burned to the ground. A story circulated that a "scalp" has been discovered by the American looters at the legislature. The "scalp" turned out to be the wig of the speaker of the house. The speaker's mace was stolen by the looters and turned up years later in a museum in Annapolis. In 1934, over 120 years after it was stolen, President F.D. Roosevelt finally agreed to return the mace to the people of Ontario.

Strachan became increasingly worried as the looters grew bolder and more aggressive. Once again, he marched to the garrison to demand an interview with Dearborn. Strachan himself had reportedly had a confrontation with two Americans, one of whom held a musket to his head. Dearborn was initially dismissive, but the letters that he sent during that time reveal that he regretted the looting. Despite those regrets, Dearborn was either unwilling or unable to rein in his men and the looting continued. Strachan continued to dog the American commander. He was especially disturbed by the story of Angelique Givins, the wife of James Givins from the Department of Indian Affairs, who told Strachan that she feared for her life. The Givins's home had been invaded by belligerent Americans who had stolen everything, including the clothing of the couple's seven children. The soldiers had threatened to shoot Angelique if she resisted. Dearborn heard the story and was sympathetic, but told Strachan there was nothing he could do to protect the wife of a man who consorted with Indians.

Commodore Chauncey was appalled to learn that the lending library had been looted and managed to track down and return two crates of books. But they were only a small part of what had been stolen. Finally, Dearborn had enough and he ordered the men back to the ships. Since York was of little strategic importance and the militia has been rendered harmless when all of the men were paroled, Dearborn had little reason to stay. Finally, on May 8th, the Americans departed.

As the sails disappeared on the horizon, Strachan and a few other men made their way to the fort to see what remained. They were distressed to find that most of the British and Canadian soldiers had been hastily buried beneath a few inches of soil. Strachan gave each man a proper burial.

In a depressingly ironic twist, Sheaffe accused the devastated townspeople of illegally taking possession of government property, including farm implements and tools that were left behind by the Americans, and demanded that they be returned.

York's defences were never restored. Instead, the town evolved into a field hospital for the Niagara front. During the worst times of the war, Strachan performed burial services for six to eight men each day, causing him to remark, "I wish that those who are so ready stirring up wars would traverse the field of battle after an engagement or visit the hospitals the next day and they would receive a lesson that might be very beneficial to them in the future."[7] Along with some of the other prominent men in York, Strachan formed the Loyal and Patriotic Society. The society was successful at soliciting funds from both sides of the Atlantic to help support wounded militiamen, war widows, and their families.

— — — —

The Americans were not completely done with York. The tiny settlement was raided again three months later, after the Americans abandoned an attempted attack on Burlington Heights. They were met with little resistance. There were no regular troops and the militia was still bound by their parole not to fight. In a few hours they burned the barracks, blockhouses, and fuel yard at the fort, opened the jail and released the inmates, made prisoners of the soldiers in the jail and hospital, and took what property they could find — both government and private. An informant revealed that there were more stores hidden up the Don River, but while several armed boats made their way upriver to find the hidden goods, a few young

Burning of the Don Bridge.

men had gone ahead of them, conveyed the goods away, and sunk the boats that had hidden them. The Americans had to content themselves with what little loot they could gather in town.

The second invasion had two immediate effects. The first was that a number of American sympathizers were tried as traitors, with Strachan's protege John Beverley Robinson serving as chief prosecutor. The second was the decision to restore and expand York's defences. Work began almost immediately and would continue until well after the war was over.

In August 1814, an American squadron caught site of the British schooner *Magnet*. Driven ashore near Fort George, the *Magnet*'s captain set the ship on fire

CANADA ON FIRE

and then blew her up to prevent her from falling into enemy hands. The American commander suspected that the *Magnet* had been sheltered in York and he decided to visit the harbour to see if there were any other prizes waiting for him there. He had one of his ships sail into York's harbour under a flag of truce to take a look before launching an attack on the fort.

York's newly paroled militiamen were not fooled. They immediately took up positions, readied the guns, and fired on the American ship. The ship momentarily returned fire before rejoining the rest of the American fleet just outside the range of York's guns. For three days the American fleet hovered menacingly just offshore. On shore, the residents of York prepared for yet another invasion. The villagers packed up their children and belongings and fled to other communities. Soldiers rose from their hospital beds to join the battle and regulars arrived from nearby garrisons to reinforce the militia. Faced with the newly reinforced defences and a militia determined not to give up the fort again, the Americans unfurled their sails and set off back across the lake.

The war lumbered on while York continued to rebuild. John Strachan would become one of Upper Canada's most powerful politicians, appointed to the executive council and to the legislative council, and one of the leaders of the infamous Family Compact whose members served as de facto rulers of Upper Canada.

What the Americans had not realized, as they sailed from York, was that the armaments and stores they had taken had been meant for the British fleet on Lake Erie. That loss would put the British fleet at such a disadvantage they would lose the battle of Lake Erie. The treatment of the citizens of York during the first invasion was not soon forgotten. Almost a year later, the British and Canadians would exact a terrible revenge with the burning of Washington, D.C.

CHAPTER EIGHT:
THE VOLTIGEURS

In the spring of 1813, with their advance into Upper Canada at a standstill, the Americans turned their attention to the less heavily defended Lower Canada. Their aim was to capture Montreal and cut off the critical British supply line from the Atlantic. They discussed their plans in detail, unaware that Canadian spies were eavesdropping and taking the information back to a young lieutenant-colonel in the British Army. This officer, a French Canadian aristocrat with the imposing name of Charles-Michel d'Irumberry de Salaberry, was aware of every plan and every move the Americans made.

De Salaberry was a career soldier both by choice and by tradition. For centuries, his forbearers had served in armies under the kings of France. When one of his ancestors moved the family to New France in the 1700s, the de Salaberrys continued their military tradition. After the British defeated the French in Lower Canada in 1759, part of the family returned to France. Those who stayed chose to give their allegiance to the French in Canada, and by extension to the British, rather than to some distant king in France. Charles's father served in various political positions with the British administration, so it was natural the family would support the British against the Americans in the War of 1812.

Charles de Salaberry was born in Beauport, Lower Canada, in 1778. He joined the British Army at age 14, serving in the West Indies and then in Holland, fighting Napoleon. His mentor and sponsor in the military was none other than the duke of Kent, the father of the future Queen Victoria. The duke spent several years in Lower Canada, where he became great friends with Charles's father.

Secrets and Spies

Despite a sparse population and the availability of only rudimentary communication tools, there were few secrets kept between the two armies during the War of 1812. Citizen spies watched from the woods and hills and eagerly reported what they had seen to their respective generals. The information supplied by Billy Green and Laura Secord helped FitzGibbon plan his defence, while David and Jacob Manning provided the details that de Salaberry needed to fend off the Americans at Châteauguay. Patriotism certainly played a role, but many of the spies were more interested in the excitement and financial reward offered by their activities.

One of the best sources of information for the British and Canadians were the American newspapers, which avidly published detailed accounts of their troop movements. The papers were eagerly read by officers in both the Canadian militia and the British Army. Many smugglers, like the Nova Scotian John Howe, took up spying as a sideline.

Even legitimate traders and diplomats were frequently used sources of information. Less than one month after the United States declared war, Sir George Prevost dispatched an affable diplomat by the name of Colonel Edward Baynes to negotiate a truce with the United States Secretary of War, Henry Dearborn. Baynes made full use of the opportunity to travel the United States unmolested while the country was preparing for war. He stopped at various forts along the way, making careful notes about the structures, troops, and ordnance that he could pass on to his superiors back in Canada.

Despite his promising military career in England, de Salaberry wanted to return to Canada and his family. He was finally transferred home in the spring of 1812, just before the war began.

De Salaberry was 34 when he returned from England, a seasoned soldier and a man to be reckoned with. He was average height, but incredibly strong and well-proportioned. For all his physical attributes, it was his personality that made him stand out from his fellow soldiers. One of de Salaberry's superiors referred to him as "my dear Marquis of cannon powder," making reference to both his aristocratic ancestry and his bold, intimidating manner. As was to be expected of a man of his background, honour meant more than life to de Salaberry — a scar on his forehead bore witness to that. While he was in Europe, a Prussian officer had bragged about killing a French Canadian. De Salaberry had told the Prussian to follow him outside so he could try to kill another. Only de Salaberry walked away from the duel.

The French Canadians were the wild card in the British deck of support. No one was really certain where their loyalty would be in the coming conflict. The Americans were counting on the French Canadians to support them. They felt the French Canadians were repressed under the British and would be anxious to escape from British "tyranny." But they were wrong. Most French Canadians disliked and distrusted American-style democracy. They were eager to protect their religion, culture, and language and the British promised those things would be protected under their administration. However, even though the French Canadians sided with the British, they resented being forcibly conscripted.

In July 1812, the British sent Governor General George Prevost to Montreal to announce the forced conscription of 2,000 bachelors into the militia. The French Canadians rose up in protest, and there was a full-fledged riot in the village of Lachine. The British soldiers rushed in. By the time they restored order, hundreds of men had been arrested and two civilians had been killed. Prevost, a far better diplomat than he was a soldier, pardoned all but the ringleaders of the riot and promised to preserve French Canadian cultural rights within the militia.

Immediately after the riots, Prevost also had the foresight to ask the dashing and popular de Salaberry to recruit and train a French Canadian militia unit they would call the Voltigeurs (the literal translation of this word is "equestrian" but de Salaberry's Voltigeurs were a light infantry, not a cavalry unit). De Salaberry drew his men from the hardiest of French Canadian stock — they were all former fur traders, trappers, and adventurers. Dressed in their distinctive grey uniforms and fur hats, the Voltigeurs were an efficient, deadly fighting force; as comfortable in the woods as they were on the battlefield. De Salaberry drilled them relentlessly until they evolved into one of Canada's best fighting units.

When Prevost first presented the idea to de Salaberry, he promised him the rank of lieutenant-colonel, a far more prestigious rank than he already held. The condition was that he had to recruit 380 men. De Salaberry's recruitment drive was wildly successful. Each recruit was offered immediate pay, along with the promise of 20 hectares of land at the completion of his service. De Salaberry upped the ante by telling his captains that they would receive no pay until they had recruited their own complement of militiamen, which was not a problem. The ranks filled quickly and de Salaberry soon had his 380 men. The wily Prevost promptly raised the minimum number of recruits to 500 men. De Salaberry was justifiably angry at the trick. However, he was a dedicated military man so he accepted the new orders. By September 1812, he had met the new quota and was given the promised reward.

De Salaberry had recruited most of the officers from among his friends and members of his large extended family. This initially posed a problem, but the officers quickly learned that the affable man who attended their balls and family parties was a very serious soldier. He would brook no disrespect and he was very firmly the man in charge. Despite, or perhaps because he was such a harsh taskmaster, he quickly earned the respect of his men. The same men who earlier in their training had complained that he was impossible to please would later become de Salaberry's most loyal admirers. His rigid training had made them into a confident fighting force, both individually and as a unit. Their growing esprit des corps was tied directly to their commander, as this Voltigeur battle songs shows:

> There's our Colonel
> With Satan in his soul
> Who'll be the death of us all
> There was no beast of prey
> That would dare stand in his way
> You'll find our Colonel is unique.

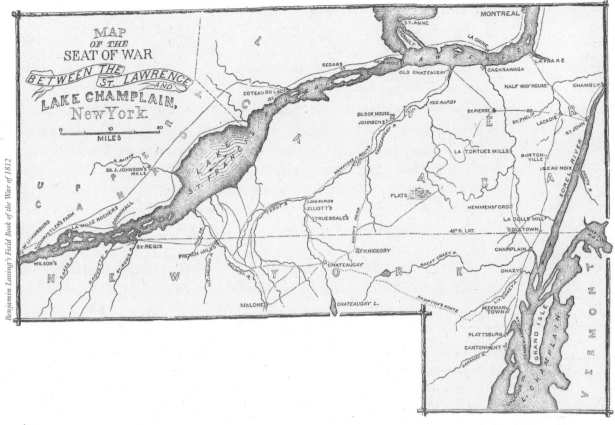

Map of the St. Lawrence River and Lake Champlain.

The Voltigeurs had decided that if de Salaberry could intimidate them, he could not help but strike terror into the hearts of their enemies. Confidence is a powerful motivator and de Salaberry was nothing if not a confident commander. Perhaps he was a little too confident.

In late November 1812, two of de Salaberry's spies, David and Jacob Manning, informed him that a large force of American troops was advancing toward the Canadian border, intending to attack Montreal. De Salaberry was so certain that the 500 Voltigeurs and Native warriors he commanded could hold off the 3,000 Americans, that he did not even bother to inform his superiors that the

Americans were on the way — an action that could have earned him a court martial. It was a telling move. De Salaberry's arrogance put him in frequent conflict with his superiors, particularly Prevost, but it was this very arrogance that made him such a deadly threat to the Americans.

De Salaberry led his men to Lacolle, a small village on the Canadian side of the Richelieu River, just north of Lake Champlain. Located about 45 kilometres south of Montreal, and a mere 20 kilometres north of the American encampment at Plattsburgh, New York, the community guarded the Richelieu River and access to the St. Lawrence River and Montreal. De Salaberry knew that Lacolle was the most likely entry point for the American force. Sure enough, in the early hours of November 27, 1812, an advance guard of about 800 American soldiers crossed Lacolle Creek. De Salaberry and his men were waiting for them in a mill, a fortified stone building.

The Voltigeurs, along with their Mohawk allies, held off the Americans for as long as they could but finally, badly outnumbered, they were forced to retreat into the surrounding forest. It was not yet dawn. The Americans, now in possession of the mill, prepared to pursue the Voltigeurs. But before they could regroup, they were attacked again. The Americans fought furiously, but when dawn broke they threw down their weapons in dismay. In the darkness and confusion, they had been fighting another unit of their own militia — a unit that had crossed the creek just hours after they had. Making use of this unexpected advantage, de Salaberry launched a counterattack. The Americans, devastated and demoralized by the recent battle with their own comrades, were too shaken to fight. They hastily retreated back across the border. Another 12 months would pass before they attempted another invasion of Lower Canada.

While the Americans were licking their wounds, de Salaberry stepped up his recruiting efforts and continued to drill his men. By the summer of 1813, he had recruited enough Voltigeurs to spare four companies — about 500 men — to help reinforce the troops fighting the Americans on the Niagara Peninsula. That summer, de Salaberry and his men also helped protect a British flotilla on Lake Champlain, providing cover while the flotilla harassed the Americans.

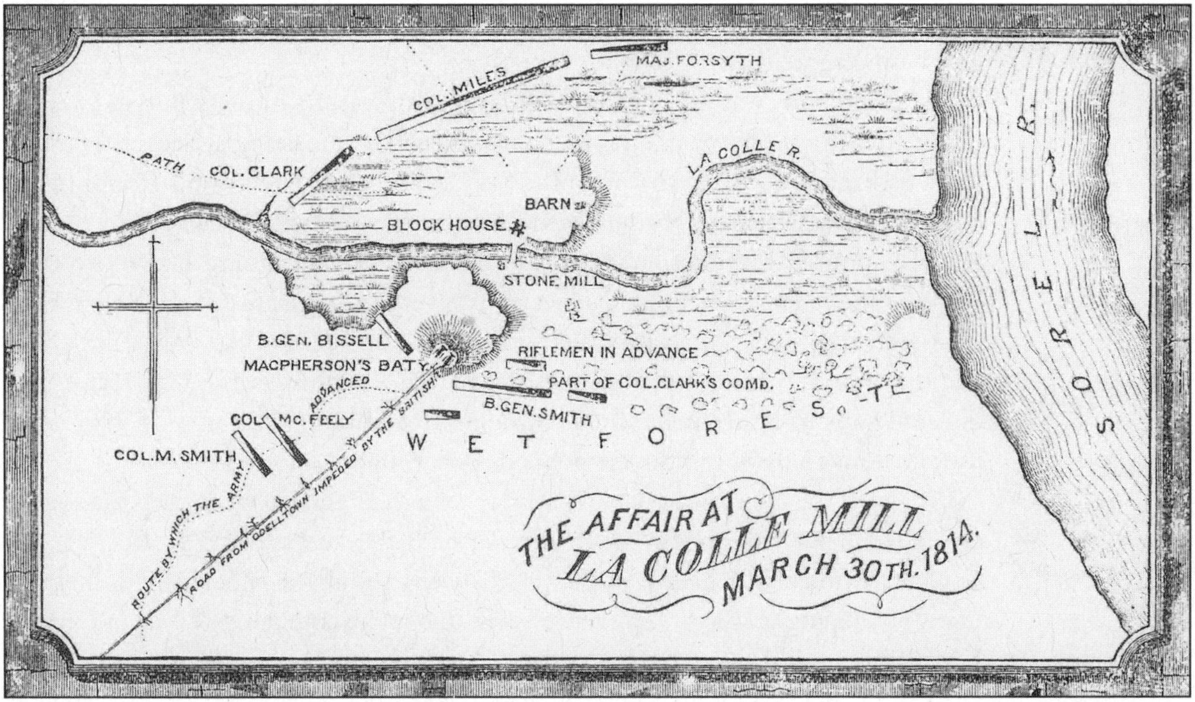
MAJ. FORSYTH
COL. MILES
PATH
COL. CLARK
LA COLLE R.
BARN
BLOCK HOUSE
STONE MILL
B.GEN. BISSELL
MACPHERSON'S BATY
RIFLEMEN IN ADVANCE
PART OF COL.CLARK'S COMD.
B.GEN.SMITH
ADVANCED
COL. MC.FEELY
COL.M. SMITH
WET FOREST
ROUTE BY WHICH THE ARMY
ROAD FROM ODELLTOWN IMPEDED BY THE BRITISH
SOREL R.
THE AFFAIR AT LA COLLE MILL MARCH 30TH. 1814.

Benjamin Lossing's Field Book of the War of 1812

The Affair at Lacolle Mills.

In the fall of 1813, the Americans were again preparing to take Montreal. Prevost knew the enemy was shifting its focus from Niagara to Lower Canada, so he ordered reinforcements. However, they would still be greatly outnumbered. Once more, the British and Canadians had to fool the Americans into believing they had huge armies. De Salaberry did this by marching his Voltigeurs from town to town and back again, much to the displeasure of the men.

In late September, the Americans began moving their troops into Lower Canada. This time, they had a sophisticated strategy: a two-pronged attack on Montreal. The plan was for one army to march along the banks of the Châteauguay River, while a second, larger force made its way up the St. Lawrence River by boat. The two rivers run parallel to each other, the Châteauguay runs slightly to the south of the St. Lawrence and the two meet a few kilometres south of Montreal. The two American armies would meet near Kahnawake, about 30 kilometres south of Montreal, to converge on the city. The invasion force was huge, numbering more than 10,000 soldiers.

The first army was led by General Wade Hampton. Its primary purpose was to divert attention from the main force that was currently massing at Sackets Harbor, New York, and preparing to sail up the St. Lawrence. As Hampton's troops headed toward the Canadian border, David Manning, a farmer who was a spy for the British, counted the guns, wagons, and soldiers. But Manning had more than mere numbers to report to de Salaberry. To everyone's surprise, 1,400 New York militiamen had refused to cross the border into Canada. By U.S. law, militiamen could not be forced to fight on foreign soil. The units from the northern states did not want to fight people they considered neighbours and friends. Nor were they anxious to be out in the elements during winter.

Many of the militia who decided to stay with their general were from the southern states. They were poorly clothed and completely unprepared to face a harsh Canadian winter. Manning also delivered details about the other American force that was heading up the St. Lawrence River under the command of Major-General James Wilkinson. De Salaberry was pleased to have learned so much. For his part, General Hampton, although furious about the loss of so many of his militia, still felt confident about the coming attack. After all, he had more than 4,000 men with him. Numbers alone should secure his victory. On September 21, he created a diversion at the town of Odelltown, just inside the Canadian border. The Americans surprised the small group of British soldiers stationed there, killing three and capturing six.

De Salaberry knew that the Americans had crossed into Canada, but the force he commanded was far too small to launch any kind of counteroffensive. The best he could do was keep the Americans contained inside Odelltown. To do that, de Salaberry sent out small units of Mohawks to intercept the American patrols. One of those units took down an American patrol. Fear of other encounters with the Native warriors kept the Americans inside the town, so they remained ignorant of how very small de Salaberry's force really was. Faced with what they believed would be a long, tough fight, and hampered by a shortage of water, Hampton once again retreated back across his own border.

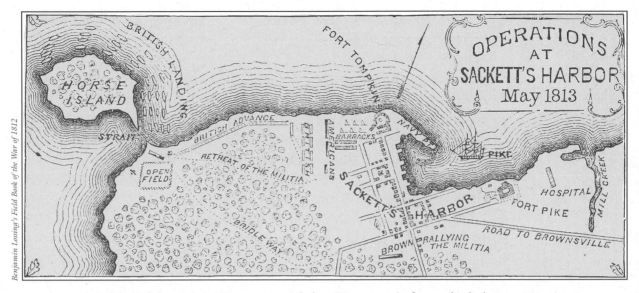

As soon as de Salaberry's scouts reported that Hampton's forces had abandoned Odelltown, de Salaberry led his men on a forced 24-hour march to the Châteauguay Valley. He knew Hampton would return and would then take his troops along this valley. The Canadian wanted to be there to greet him. De Salaberry left detachments of soldiers along the way to serve as communication outposts. He finally reached the valley, where he set up camp and waited for Hampton.

Meanwhile, Hampton had set up camp at Four Corners, a small town just inside the American border at the southern end of the Châteauguay Valley, about 15 kilometres from de Salaberry's camp. When de Salaberry learned of the Americans' whereabouts from his spies, he sent a few units of warriors and Voltigeurs to pepper the encampment with sniper fire. They terrorized the camp every night for two weeks. The Americans were so alarmed that they would not venture outside the encampment at night.

On October 1, de Salaberry received orders from Prevost to raid the encampment. It seemed like a suicide mission — de Salaberry's several hundred Voltigeurs and warriors against Hampton's several thousand militiamen. De Salaberry

Operations at Sackets Harbor.

THE VOLTIGEURS

127

later wrote to his father that he suspected Prevost was trying to get rid of him. In spite of that, de Salaberry followed orders and stormed the camp.

The Americans quickly recovered from their surprise and launched a massive counterattack. During this attack, the Mohawks withdrew twice. Both times, de Salaberry brought them back. But on the third withdrawal, they were gone for good, taking a number of Voltigeurs with them. Only de Salaberry and four of his men were left to fend off the Americans. When night fell, the five exhausted men were able to slip away. Further attacks would be out of the question.

De Salaberry returned to his camp. He knew that Hampton's plans had not changed and that he and his men would soon be marching along the banks of the Châteauguay River to join up with the other invading force at Kahnawake. He took his men along the same route and ordered them to destroy bridges and push felled trees across the path behind them. The young lieutenant-colonel was determined not to allow Hampton to reach Kahnawake, so he searched for a suitable area to make a stand against the huge force. Finally, at a series of sharp ravines where the English River flows into the Châteauguay, de Salaberry found his battlefield. The thick bush, blocked roads, and burned bridges had slowed Hampton's troops, giving de Salaberry the precious time he needed to prepare. His men fortified the ravines with "abatis," felled trees piled atop one another with their tops pointing downward.

In the meantime, Prevost, who was in Kingston, had finally realized that Montreal was the Americans' main target. He made plans to take reinforcements to de Salaberry by land. But first he sent for Lieutenant-Colonel "Red George" Macdonnell and asked him to take a battalion to de Salaberry by boat. The soldiers hastily rounded up some boats and set off from Kingston on the treacherous St. Lawrence River. They were caught in a blinding storm but forged on. The men reached de Salaberry 60 hours later, an incredibly short time for having to travel a distance of more than 200 kilometres in such difficult conditions.

Red George reached de Salaberry on October 24. Although de Salaberry was pleased to see the reinforcements he knew the extra numbers would not ensure victory. They were still outnumbered three to one. It was time to try another bluff. By this time, Hampton's troops were very close. Close enough to see what they thought were hundreds of reinforcements marching toward de Salaberry's camp. De Salaberry had used Brock's ploy of having the same men march back and forth wearing what looked like different uniforms each time. Not actually having any different uniforms, the men just turned their jackets inside out so the white lining showed. Hampton was fooled into believing de Salaberry's force was twice the size of his own. Therefore, he dismissed the idea of a head-on assault. Instead, on October 25, 1813, he sent a force of 1,500 men into the forests to attack de Salaberry's flanks. The Voltigeur scouts detected them. Red George and his men, along with a group of Voltigeurs, engaged the Americans and fought them off.

That afternoon, Hampton decided he would have to try a head-on assault after all. The American troops advanced toward the ravines. De Salaberry fired the first shot. There was a furious exchange of fire and de Salaberry ordered his men to take cover behind the abatis. Believing that the Canadians and British were retreating, the Americans began to cheer. De Salaberry encouraged his men to return the victory shouts. These shouts came from the top of every ravine. Then Red George's men picked up the shouts from their reserve position in the woods. The Mohawks added to the ruckus with their war whoops. The Americans finally stopped cheering. They fired volley after volley into the woods at what they believed were thousands of warriors. Finally, to add to the ruse and American confusion, de Salaberry sent his buglers into the woods to sound an imaginary advance.

Silence fell over both armies. De Salaberry called out to one of his Voltigeurs in French, warning him to communicate solely in French so that the enemy would not understand. The man replied that the soldiers who had attacked their flanks that morning had regrouped and were attacking again. De Salaberry told him to draw the fight to the riverbank. When the Americans reached the river, they were met by more Voltigeurs and a barrage of fire. This was enough to send the entire American force into disarray. They hastily retreated back into the forest. Hampton, outsmarted by his enemy once more, ordered a general withdrawal. In the haste to retreat, the American dead and wounded were left in the ravines. De

Salaberry had the American wounded taken to a nearby field hospital, along with his own wounded.

Following the American retreat, de Salaberry's men immediately set to work repairing the battlements. De Salaberry only expected to gain some time with his bluffs before the Americans would return. He had not realized that he had won a decisive and complete victory. De Salaberry and his men spent the next eight days huddled against the abatis while a storm raged around them, waiting for an enemy who would never return. Exposed to the elements, they were utterly miserable. One of the Voltigeurs wrote,

> We suffered so much from … foul weather that some of our men fell sick every day. I now know that a man could endure without dying more pain and hell than a dog. There were many things that I could tell you easier than I could write them, but you would be convinced by this affair that Canadians know how to fight.[1]

While General Hampton was leading his troops back to the border, the other arm of the American invasion force, 7,000 men strong, was making its way up the St. Lawrence River in hundreds of light river boats. The flotilla made slow progress. From the Canadian side of the river they were bombarded by a constant stream of cannon fire, and their commander, General Wilkinson, was sick and in no state to rally his troops. The soldiers were not in a hurry to go anywhere. It took them eight days to cover 130 kilometres. Along the way, the American flotilla stopped to interrogate farmers on both sides of the border, hoping to get intelligence about the British and Canadian forces. The soldiers also looted the homes and property of Canadian civilians, behaviour that earned them the lasting hatred of the local population. When the Americans interrogated them, the Canadians fed them a series of outrageous tales that magnified the strength of everything from the rapids ahead to the size of the army they would face. This time, it was the civilians who tricked the Americans into believing they were up against a huge army.

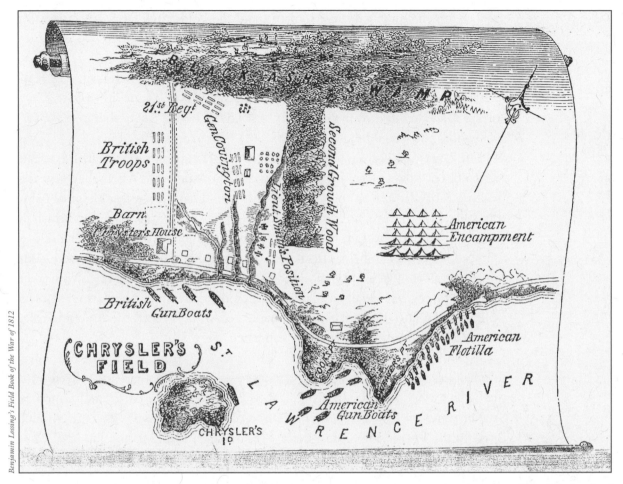

Benjamin Lossing's Field Book of the War of 1812

Finally, on November 11, 1813, the American force reached a farm owned by a man named John Chrysler. They knew they could go no farther by boat until they had disabled the cannons that were still firing at them from the Canadian side of the river. The dangerous Long Sault Rapids were ahead, and they could not hope to navigate them while under fire. The Canadians and British had expected the Americans to stop at Chrysler's farm. They told the Chrysler family to hide in their cellar, and then positioned their troops in the surrounding fields. There were

Map of the Battle of Chrysler's Field.

units of British regulars, Native warriors, and the Voltigeurs. De Salaberry wasn't there. He'd led his men to the next battle after realizing that there would be no more action on the Châteauguay.

As always, the defending army was vastly outnumbered. Therefore, they scattered in small groups: a unit of Voltigeurs in the woods, a unit of Mohawks in a cornfield, and a unit of British regulars beyond the barns. Everywhere the Americans looked, they could see the enemy.

The Americans had already received word of Hampton's demoralizing defeat. His troops would not be joining the attack on Montreal. When they saw the troops at Chrysler's farm, they realized they would have to engage them. Wilkinson, still too ill to leave his bed, ordered his junior officer to engage the British in a standard military fashion, fighting first one unit and then the next. The officer followed his orders and the effects were debilitating. The Americans were continually harassed. Just as they appeared to dispatch one unit of the enemy, another stood up to engage. Finally, Wilkinson called the retreat. The exhausted soldiers willingly piled into their boats and retreated across the river to the American side. The attack on Montreal never really happened.

After the twin battles of Chrysler's Farm and Châteauguay, Prevost attempted to take credit for the Châteauguay victory, even though he had not arrived until the battle was all but over. In his official correspondence, he barely mentioned de Salaberry and the Voltigeurs, other than to claim that they served as the advance force for the British. Of course, there were many witnesses to the Battle of Châteauguay, and they wanted the truth to be known. Accurate accounts of the battle appeared in the *Montreal Gazette*. Even de Salaberry, normally reticent about his achievements, was angry enough to send his own accounts of the battle back to the high command in Britain. As it turned out, the high command had not been fooled by Prevost's claims. The legislature in Lower Canada congratulated de Salaberry on his victory and a representative of the Prince Regent made special mention of de Salaberry and the Voltigeurs in his official remarks about the battle.

De Salaberry was too busy to bother himself much over Prevost's fiction. His men were exhausted; they had been on the move since early September and needed some rest. Late in November, Prevost ordered them to stage a hopeless raid on the American encampment at Four Corners, New York, where they had almost been annihilated two months earlier.

It seemed like a pointless endeavour, but de Salaberry dutifully led 300 of his men back to Four Corners. It was cold and raining. After a miserable night in a makeshift camp, the men awoke covered in frost. They also awoke to the news that one of their scouts was missing. They reasoned he had probably been captured while reconnoitering the enemy camp. The scout who did return reported that a large contingent of Americans was waiting for them with heavy gun support. Ever the gifted poker player, de Salaberry knew when to bluff; he also knew when to fold. With an unwinnable hand, and no options, he withdrew.

Plagued by rheumatism and fevers from his long military service, de Salaberry considered retirement. But in January 1814, he received orders to head off a possible American attack on Coteau-du-Lac. He hastily called up 600 Voltigeurs and some of the 49th Regiment. They marched the 60 kilometres to Coteau-du-Lac, losing two dozen men to frostbite along the way. When they got there, they realized it was a false alarm. There were no Americans, and no impending attack. De Salaberry returned to Montreal in February, ill and disillusioned.

When he was offered a lateral transfer that would take him out of direct fighting, de Salaberry accepted. But when an American force again massed along the border of Lower Canada, he was tempted back into active service. Together, he and his Voltigeurs defeated the invasion force. By that time, de Salaberry had definitely had enough of military service. He was 36 and had been at war for more than half his life. He was a married man and wanted to enjoy the pleasures of a more peaceful, domesticated life. He sent an official letter to the Duke of Kent, requesting leave to retire. His mentor refused to process his request. A peace was being negotiated and the duke felt the war would soon be over. If de Salaberry could hold out for a few more months, he would be able to retire with the half-pay that was due to all officers who served the entire length of the war. De Salaberry decided to stay the course.

As the war drew to a close, Charles-Michel de Salaberry received accolades from his men, his generals, and his country. In 1818, he was appointed to the legislative council of Lower Canada. Years later, when most British civilians had forgotten the War of 1812, he was made a Companion of the Order of Bath.

CHAPTER NINE:
THE SEA WOLVES

When the war began, the British Navy was considered the best and largest in the world. With hundreds of vessels at its disposal it was virtually invincible. Although many ships were already engaged patrolling the waters around Britain and blockading the French, 85 vessels were patrolling in or near the eastern coast of North America. The American Navy, on the other hand, was virtually nonexistent, consisting of no more than 22 commissioned vessels.

But what the Americans lacked in numbers they made up for in size and firepower. Their ships tended to be larger, the three main U.S. warships carried 44 guns each and each of those guns was much heavier than the 24-pounders found on a typical British warship. Though they struggled to find their footing on land, the Americans found relatively easy victories on the water. Worried British commanders immediately commissioned construction of five new warships. It was to this precarious situation that a battle-hardened, career seaman named Sir James Yeo was sent. His new title was certainly prestigious: commodore and commander-in-chief of the British Navy on the Canadian Great Lakes. In reality, Yeo was taking control of a very small group of vessels that roamed a tightly compacted group of lakes split evenly between two countries that were engaged in a violent war.

If anyone was up to the task of preventing the Americans from taking control of the lakes it was Yeo. He had entered the British Navy at the age of 10, and within four years had attained the rank of lieutenant. Yeo quickly developed a reputation for coolness and daring. He led two dramatic operations that resulted in the defeat of a much larger force than his own. During the first operation he helped rescue the Portuguese royal family and during the second he helped drive the French from South America. For the latter he was knighted by the Portuguese and a few years later he received a British knighthood as well.

Yeo arrived in Canada a few days after York had fallen to the Americans. His Canadian position offered a much different challenge, requiring caution and patience rather than daring and quick-wittedness.

While Canadian privateers harried the east coast and the British Navy maintained a tight blockade on the Atlantic coast, it was the Americans who dominated the inland water. By 1813, the Americans had Lake Erie in a stranglehold, with a seemingly unbreakable blockade at Amherstburg on the Detroit River. When Sir James Yeo sailed into Lake Ontario to assume his new position as commodore and commander-in-chief of the British Navy in the Canadian Great Lakes, he immediately decided that he needed to concentrate his attention on Lake Ontario. Lake Erie was expendable, Lake Ontario, which served as a vital supply line for troops on the Niagara frontier, was not. His philosophy left the Lake Erie force chronically short of ships, men, and supplies. The American blockade made the situation much worse. Food supplies at Amherstburg were running out and there was no more money to pay the army. Sailors had been put at half-rations.

The first major attempt by the British to regain control of the lakes ended in defeat at Sackets Harbor. At the time, the American Navy was preoccupied with supporting a raid on Fort George. The British commanders saw an opportunity to attack the American naval base at Sackets Harbor. They planned to burn the newly completed American frigate *General Pike*. The British lay anchor several kilometres offshore and the soldiers quickly climbed into flat-bottom boats to make their way to shore. They had gone only a little way before Prevost thought he saw ships in the distance and, fearing the return of the main American fleet, called the soldiers back. It was a false alarm but Prevost still refused to remount the attack until the next morning. This gave the Americans time to call out the militia.

Finally, the British naval and army commanders at Fort Erie, Robert Barclay and Henry Proctor, felt that they had no choice but to break through the American blockade. The battle of Lake Erie raged for four violent hours, with devastating losses on both sides, before the British finally surrendered. For the first time in

the over 300-year history of the British Navy, one of its fleets had been completely defeated. The American response to the victory was surprisingly understated. "We have met the enemy," wrote Oliver Hazard Perry, "and they are ours." The defeat forced the British and Canadians to abandon Fort Amherstburg, leaving the field open to William Henry Harrison, who quickly launched an invasion and pursued Proctor all the way up the Thames River. For months afterward, the Americans would dominate Lake Erie.

James Yeo believed that his naval commanders in Lake Erie, and later in the Battle of Chesapeake Bay, had been forced into action before they were ready by army commanders who outranked them but knew little of the intricacies of naval warfare. He was determined not to let the same thing happen in Lake Ontario. He also knew that he did not necessarily have to take Lake Ontario, he simply had to ensure that the Americans did not take it either. As long as the supply lines remained open he could consider his efforts a success. There was a lot at stake. The loss of Lake Ontario would practically assure the loss of Canada, so Yeo's first

The Battle of Lake Erie.

priority was to ensure he had the fleet to protect the lake. He immediately ordered the launch of an ambitious shipbuilding program, which would eventually produce several ships, including the near mythical HMS *St. Lawrence*, a mammoth 104-gun frigate that would be one of the largest ships in the world.

Yeo still faced a number of challenges. The Americans had better, more easily accessible supply and communication lines, and with the British blockade of the Atlantic coast keeping American ships in port, they had more resources in general. Most of their ocean-going ships were sailing the inland waters. Kingston was chronically short of shipbuilders and dockyard workers, and the shipment of raw materials up the St. Lawrence River was both expensive and dangerous. A mild winter had made land transportation problematic. Still, Yeo forged ahead with his ambitious plans. While the *St. Lawrence* was still under construction in Kingston, Yeo played a game of virtual one-upmanship with his American counterpart, Commodore Chauncey. Each had spies delivering news of the other's shipbuilding efforts. Occasionally they would engage in minor skirmishes, but no major victory was scored by either side. Citizens on both sides of the lake would frequently see small convoys of ships from the American and British navies, sailing up and down the lake. But whether the ships were posturing or performing some of kind of reconnaissance, the citizens could not be sure. On September 26, 1813, the few people who happened to be strolling along the cliffs of Burlington Heights would see something much more intriguing.

That morning dawned cloudy and cool. A brisk breeze blew, warning of more volatile weather to come later in the day. There was dampness in the air, too. Nevertheless, Yeo and his fleet of six ships made their way out onto the lake. From their home on the other side of the lake, Commodore Chauncey and nine of his ships slipped out of their berth and made their way toward the British fleet. For most of the morning, the two fleets danced and darted in various positions on the lake, before stepping cautiously out of danger. Finally, as the midday sun struggled to find its way out of the clouds, the two opposing navies lined up into battle formation. Chauncey was under great pressure. Only 18 days before, his subordinate had scored an incredible victory in Lake Erie, but it was useless

without a corresponding victory in Lake Ontario. And Chauncey's latest ship, the *Pike*, was ready to sail. With the HMS *St. Lawrence* still under construction, and having fewer ships than his American counterpart, all Yeo needed to do was to avoid handing Chauncey a win. A draw could do no damage.

While the Americans outgunned the British, the British ships were lighter and more easily manoeuvered. They also had Yeo's many years of experience on their side. He ordered his ships into a formation that forced the Americans to split and lengthen their own formation, limiting the use of their guns and exposing their flagship, the *Pike*, to British fire. Then, after ordering his men to take aim for the *Pike*'s

Boarding and Taking of the American Ship Chesapeake by the Officers and Crew of the Shannon.

THE SEA WOLVES

hull, Yeo yelled at them to fire. For the next four hours, a fierce battle raged. The *Pike* was listing badly from a cannonball ripping a hole in her hull below the waterline. Another cannonball exploded on her deck, sending sailors and gunners into the air and the lake. Yeo's ship, the *Wolfe*, withstood the heaviest American fire. Its sails were shredded and, with an ear splitting crash, its topmast and mizzen-mast were both cut in two by cannon fire. The ship listed pathetically, paralyzed by the damage it had sustained and struggling to defend itself from a strengthening American attack.

A collective gasp rippled through the swelling group of spectators on the Heights. Surely Yeo was finished and Lake Ontario was lost. But Yeo was not ready to strike his colours. He ordered his ships around and they set sail. They raced down the lake and soon Chauncey's ships were in hot pursuit. To the people on the Heights, the pursuit had all the appearances of a friendly yacht race and it later became known in local yore as the Burlington Races. Numerous myths grew up around the Races. It was even said that the intrepid Yeo had navigated the maze of sandbars near Burlington through less than four feet of water to reach the safety of the harbour there. The myths were just that, myths, but Yeo did have a plan. He planned to engage "on more equal terms" in the relative safety of the Burlington shore, just beneath the power guns on the Heights. He laid anchor with a system of ropes that allowed his ship to slide back and forth, presenting fresh guns to the enemy each time. His other ships did the same. They waited for the Americans to re-form and attack.

To nearly everyone's surprise, Chauncey and his ships approached and then abruptly turned back to their home port across the lake. The *Pike* had been more badly damaged than the *Wolfe* and Chauncey did not dare attack Yeo while he remained under the protection of Burlington's guns. A great cheer went up on the ships, which was quickly echoed on the Heights behind them. The British fleet limped back into Kingston for repairs. Yeo would make good use of the reprieve for the next few months, maintaining a blockade at Sackets Harbor and protecting the mouth of the St. Lawrence River. When his great ship, the *St. Lawrence*, was launched, it was clear that Yeo had won the arms race on the great lakes. For the remainder of the war, the British fleet controlled Lake Ontario.

Yeo was summoned back to London to present a report to the British high command. His report was characteristically blunt. Any successes the British had enjoyed on the Great Lakes were due in large part to the colossal "stupidity" of the American commanders there. The war might easily have been won by the Americans had they managed to shut down the British supply line on the St. Lawrence. He further warned that the Americans were not likely to make the same mistake twice and that "the preservation of Canada by means of a naval force on the lakes will, in my opinion, be an endless, if not futile undertaking."[1] To aid in the colony's defence, Yeo suggested the building of a new supply line via a water route between Kingston and Montreal. That suggestion would eventually lead the creation of the Rideau Canal.[2]

When Yeo took his leave of the port of Kingston, the city magistrates gathered to provide him with a public address recognizing his contributions in defence of Canada and their thanks. When he debarked a few days later in Montreal, the fathers of that city presented him with a sword worth over 500 pounds sterling.

— — — —

While Yeo was jockeying for position on Lake Ontario in the late summer of 1814, three very different men were meeting aboard a ship at the mouth of the Potomac River. All three were British, all three were military men, but that's where the similarities ended. One was an Irish-born army man, the others were attached to the British Navy — one an Irishman, the other a Scotsman. They were united by a special assignment. Together they would hatch a plan to divert American attention from the other theatres of war and exact revenge for the American looting of York.

Robert Ross was the sole soldier in the group. A veteran of the Napoleonic Wars who had been wounded three times, General Ross had just arrived in North America at the head of a group of 4,500 battle-hardened fellow veterans. Although he was known to be a strict disciplinarian, he easily commanded the loyalty of his men. They knew that he would not send them anywhere that he was not willing to go himself, and that when they met the enemy he would be in the thick of the battle with them.

The leader of the group, Admiral Alexander Cochrane, would command the operation. An experienced commander and former governor of Guadeloupe, Admiral Cochrane had been appointed as head of the North American station for the British Navy in 1814. One of his first acts was to declare that any Americans could choose to join the British Army or Navy, or be relocated to live as free settlers in the British possessions in North America or the West Indies. The proclamation was aimed directly at the slave population around the Chesapeake Bay. Cochrane then set up a base on Tangier Island, close to the Chesapeake. Runaway slaves flocked there for sanctuary and the British offered them employment as messengers, guides, and pilots.

Many of these former slaves wanted to perform more active service in the war effort and soon Cochrane ordered his subordinate, Admiral George Cockburn, to form three companies of a new Corps of Colonial Marines from the groups of runaway slaves. Cockburn was initially skeptical that this ragtag bunch of runaways could help the war effort, but he soon admitted his error. They were, he would later report, "excellent men," talented and resourceful soldiers. Ross agreed, pointing to their "spirit and vivacity" along with their particular aptitude for skirmishing. They never deserted and never refused an order. Cockburn would even insist that several of the Colonial Marines accompany him on his own ship as he considered them stronger and more trustworthy than the regular marines who accompanied him.

As the three men sat around the rough wooden table in the captain's quarters of Cochrane's ship they certainly considered the Colonial Marines in their plans. Just over 500 men served in the Marines and most would be present at the battle to come. It is unclear exactly how many slaves escaped to find refuge with the British and Canadians during the war, but a postwar commission suggested the number exceeded 3,000 men, women, and children. Although they were offered a permanent commission in the British Army, they refused, and many settled in Nova Scotia at the close of the war.

Cochrane was determined to create havoc on the American Atlantic coast and he ordered numerous raids, particularly in the Chesapeake Bay area. When George Prevost ordered him to ratchet up the pressure on the coast, Cochrane ordered the destruction of American towns. One of his first victims was the town of Nantucket. There he forced the town fathers to agree to a neutral position and to withhold their federal taxes in exchange for Cochrane not destroying the town. Cochrane's main weapon in the Chesapeake was Rear-Admiral George Cockburn, who would prove to be a formidable weapon. By the time of the shipboard meeting, Admiral Cockburn was probably the most hated man in the U.S. The American newspapers and taverns teemed with tales of the numerous outrages he had committed against the American people in the Chesapeake.

Like Yeo, George Cockburn was just 10 years old when he joined the Royal Navy as a midshipman. He rose quickly through the ranks and was given command of his first ship at the age of 20. He became friendly with Horatio Nelson and was one of the heroes of the Napoleonic Wars. He also amassed a huge private fortune from the many French and Spanish ships he captured. Cockburn could easily have retired comfortably on his winnings, but the call to adventure was strong and when a new war was declared in North America, Cockburn did not take long to join it. Few Americans had even heard of George Cockburn when he first appeared at the edge of Chesapeake Bay in 1813. Before the year was out they would all wish they had never heard of him.

Like a terrifying storm, Cockburn's small fleet darted in and out of the bay, raiding and burning towns in his path. His purpose was as simple as it was brutal. If the communities along the coast were introduced to the brutalities of war, they might be less inclined to lend their support to their country's invasion of Canada. Cockburn's ships raided port after port. In Lynnhaven Bay they captured a collection of boats. A few days later, in Frenchtown, they destroyed stores of food and supplies intended for the American Army. When the raids began, the towns along the coast remained defiant. As he sailed past the tiny town of Havre de Grace, Cockburn noticed the Stars and Stripes flying over the town battery. Incensed, he ordered his men to shore, jumping into the first boat to lead the raid himself. The red glare of the Congreve rockets that were fired by Cockburn's men lit up the grey dawn and forced most of the residents out of town. Only one elderly Irishman remained and he stubbornly manned the battery against the British attack. Cockburn was so impressed with the old man that he ordered him captured rather than killed and promptly released the old man into British hands. But Cockburn was not yet done with the town. Forty of the town's 60 homes were burnt to the ground before he and his troops took their leave.

Finding little resistance to his raiding, Cockburn became even bolder. He took his men and ships up the Sassafras River. When several of his sailors were wounded by sniper fire he ordered the destruction of the villages of Georgetown and Fredericktown.

Across the United States, newspapers railed against the brutality of the man they called "Cock BURN." He was labelled a bully, vandal, bandit, and savage. He may have been hated by the Americans but Cockburn was motivated purely by his sense of duty. He did not hate the Americans, he was simply determined to defeat them. While he had a "sincere desire to lessen to individuals the hardships inseparable from war,"[3] he also had a firm concept of what constituted fairness in war. He detested the guerrilla style practiced by the Americans and was capable of inflicting harsh punishments on those who opposed him. He was just as capable of allowing those who did not resist to remain free. He always offered compensation for the goods he appropriated and allowed the people of the Chesapeake the freedom to travel and fish on the bay. He even allowed some captured ships to go free when he learned that their capture would place undue hardship on the owners.

But the American press only saw his barbarity. When he received a promotion, his ships fired a salute from their canons. After watching the spectacle, the editor of a Baltimore newspaper caustically noted that "the ruffian (Cockburn) will be anxious to deserve this distinction, by some act of great atrocity and meanness, or we much mistake his character."[4]

By the spring of 1814 Cockburn had established an almost mechanical approach to his raids. After landing his marines in a targeted town, he would send out buglers in all directions. If they met resistance, they'd use their horns and summon Cockburn, who would ensure the town paid for their opposition. A single shot from an errant patriot was enough to make Cockburn order an entire town burned and looted. If no resistance occurred, Cockburn would ensure that the town remained unmolested and its people were compensated for any goods taken by his men.

As Cockburn, Ross, and Cochrane met at the mouth of the Potomac to consider their options in the spring of 1814, Cockburn was confident that the entire bay was his for the taking. If the British high command wanted a distraction that would divert attention from the Niagara front he could provide a magnificent one. He pressed for an immediate attack on no less than Washington, D.C., itself. Cochrane, despite his derision for all things American and his intention to "give them a good drubbing,"[5] was less certain of victory. Such an attack would most certainly force the Americans to redirect troops from Niagara to Washington, but Washington was upriver and attacking it would both isolate and expose British troops. Should the mission fail they were in danger of being completely cut off.

Instead, Cochrane gave orders to Ross and Cockburn to locate and destroy a small fleet of American ships that had found refuge on the Patuxent River under the direction of the Commodore Joshua Barney. But Cochrane was not about to give up the plan he had been nurturing for the better part of the last year. To divert attention and confuse the enemy, he sent part of his fleet up the Potomac. Another part of the fleet was dispatched across the Chesapeake to a point just above Baltimore. On August 20th, he and Ross led the remainder — a formidable force of nearly 4,000 seasoned soldiers, sailors, and marines — up the Patuxent to look for Commodore Barney. Barney was an experienced former privateer and he knew immediately that he was trapped. Several British ships blocked his exit from the Patuxent while thousands of British troops were already moving up the shore to find him. The British troops, led by Ross, moved slowly upriver burdened by heavy packs, guns, and a load of large Congreve rockets. Alongside them on the river, Cockburn led his flotilla of barges, rafts, and small boats filled with sailors and marines. Barney and his fleet continued to withdraw upstream until the shallows forced them to stop.

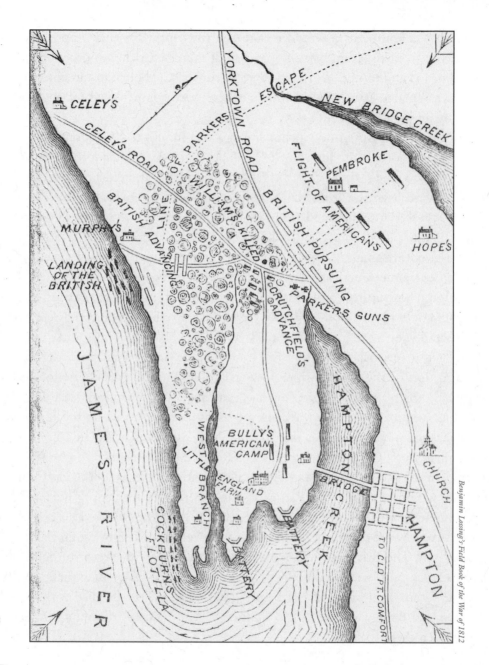

The labels within the map image read:

CELEY'S

YORKTOWN ROAD

ESCAPE

NEW BRIDGE CREEK

CELEY'S ROAD

PARKERS ROAD

FLIGHT OF AMERICANS

PEMBROKE

WILLIAMS KILLED

BRITISH ADVANCING LINE

BRITISH PURSUING

HOPE'S

MURPHY'S

LANDING OF THE BRITISH

PARKERS GUNS

CRUTCHFIELD'S ADVANCE

JAMES RIVER

HAMPTON CREEK

CHURCH

BULLY'S AMERICAN CAMP

WEST LITTLE BRANCH

ENGLAND FARM

BATTERY

BRIDGE

HAMPTON

TO OLD PT. COMFORT

COCKBURNS FLOTILLA

Benjamin Lossing's Field Book of the War of 1812

Map of the Chesapeake Bay area.

Within Washington confusion reigned. President Madison was convinced that the capital was Cockburn's intended target, but others in the government — namely Secretary of War John Armstrong — were convinced the capital was safe. Washington presented no strategic or military advantage and Armstrong could see no real purpose in the British attacking it. Besides, it was too far upriver for the British to risk exposing their troops. Armstrong did not assign any regular troops to guard the capital. Instead, the government had to rely on the local militia, who could only be called up in the event of an attack or other imminent disaster. The man in charge of the defence — General John Winder — scurried about, collecting what militia he could and receiving the reports of scouts who had been sent out to determine the British purpose.

On August 21, Cockburn finally caught up with Barney's flotilla only to find it already in flames. The pragmatic Barney had set fire to his ships and retreated to Washington to offer his assistance in the defence of the city. Cockburn was quick to follow. Leaving his ships in the shallow waters of the Patuxent, he joined Ross. Ross was ready to return to Canada. The mission set by Cochrane was complete, but Washington lay less than 32 kilometres away and Cockburn could not let the prize go when it was still so close. He pressed his case and managed to convince Ross to continue. Once he had decided on a course, even a command from Cochrane to give up on Washington could not make Cockburn change his mind. Using his prerogative as ranking officer in the field, he ordered his men to press on.

Cockburn's troops marched for kilometres until they had halved the distance between them and Washington. Still, no army came out to meet them. Could it be that they would march into the American capital completely unopposed? Within Washington itself, the people were in a panic. It was clear to virtually everyone that the British were headed for their city. People packed up their belongings and prepared to flee before the impending fight. Someone took the Constitution and the Declaration of Independence and hid them in the loft of a grist mill on the edge of town. Dolly Madison, wife of the president, was also being urged to flee but she refused until a portrait of General Washington could be removed and added to the wagon with her belongings. Just as Joshua Barney and his sailors made their way into Washington, General Winder had finally reached the inevitable conclusion: he would have to lead his reluctant, green troops out to meet the enemy.

Barney, who had been ordered to stay in Washington to protect the Navy Yard, had little faith that the men Winder led would be able to hold off the British. They were too undisciplined, too inexperienced. Winder himself offered his troops instructions for retreat — long before they even reached the battlefield. Some people had faith. A young militia private, perhaps thrilled by the adventure he was about to take part in, recorded in his journal that the people of Washington lined the streets to cheer on their troops "as we hurried along in brisk step to familiar music, with banners fluttering in the wind and bayonets flashing in the sun."[6] Inside his kit the young private had also packed a set of dress shoes. If the president invited them to a ball after the day's business was over, he wanted to be ready for it.

Finally the two armies met near the small town of Bladensburg. Winder split his troops into three groups. One defended the road to Washington and the others guarded their flanks. Despite his reservations about Winder's men, Barney did not want to be left behind. He argued that he be allowed to take his men into battle and was finally given permission. They reached Bladensburg just as the two armies engaged. Overhead, the Congreve rockets screeched and flashed, causing little damage but striking fear into the hearts of the Americans. Faced with the relentless charge of the British regulars, the American militia broke. Barney and his men kept up a steady stream of fire on the approaching British, cutting down dozens of them, but it did not stop the advance. Lacking the training to retreat in any kind of organized form, and forgetting Winder's instructions, the Americans turned and ran back toward Washington in a legendary retreat that became known as the Bladensburg Races.

Ross would later remark that the Americans had retreated too quickly for the British to even take any prisoners. Cockburn was thrilled with the easy victory but the real prize was just down the road. He rode up on his white charger, with gold laced hat and epaulettes, sidestepping through the wounded and dead on the Bladensburg Road. He came across a wounded Joshua Barney, who

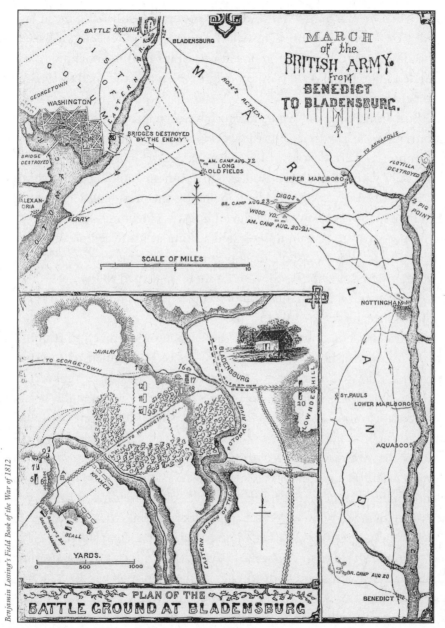

Map of the British Army's route to the battlefield at Bladensburg.

shrugged when he saw him. "Well, Admiral, you have got hold of me at last," he observed. Cockburn was impressed with the courage and tenacity of Barney and before heading toward Washington he left one of his own men behind to care for the wounded man. It was 4:00 p.m. on August 24th and the road to Washington lay open before them.

The British marched on, expecting to have their progress challenged by the militia or regulars at any time. But the woods remained silent, the few structures they encountered were devoid of life. Even as they reached the city itself, they were met only with silence. The houses, government buildings, and shops had all been abandoned. Everyone had fled, including the president. Cochrane, Ross, and their men made their way slowly through town. Cochrane's orders were clear. Private property was to remain unmolested as long as it offered no opposition to the British troops. When a couple of snipers took aim at his men, Cockburn, true to his word, ordered the houses they took refuge in burned to the ground. Seeing the flames, the handful of American sailors who remained at the Navy Yard set the yard and its ships ablaze, then fled.

One of the first buildings Cockburn came upon on his march through Washington was the unfinished Capitol building. There he climbed to the speaker's platform and addressed his men. "Shall we burn this harbour of Yankee Democracy?"[7] he asked. The soldiers and marines yelled out a resounding "aye," and then proceeded to loot and burn the building, using books from the Library of Congress to fuel the fire. Cockburn himself took the copy of *An Account of the Receipts and Expenditures for the United States for the Year 1810* just to prove he had been in Madison's office. Next, Cockburn and his men made their way to the presidential mansion where they found the table still set for dinner, drinks poured. Cockburn encouraged his men to take souvenirs and while they looted, he settled into one of the comfortable leather dining chairs, lit a cigar, lifted a glass, and toasted "Jemmie's" (Madison's) health. Ross gathered furniture for kindling and Cockburn had his men stand with torches at the mansions windows. On Cockburn's order, they threw the torches through the window and in an instant the entire mansion was in flames.

CANADA ON FIRE

The Attack on Fort Washington

While Admiral Cochrane was launching his attack on Washington, another naval officer — Captain James Alexander Gordon — was slowly making his way up the Potomac with a handful of ships and less than one thousand men. His objective was Fort Washington but his purpose was to act as a decoy to draw attention away from Admiral Cochrane's forces and the main attack.

On the night of August 24, 1914, Gordon and his troops watched as the sky suddenly lit up. There could be no mistaking the glow; Washington was on fire. A cheer went up among the troops and it seemed that there was no longer any reason for them to continue, but Gordon had other ideas. He ordered the flotilla to continue on toward Fort Washington and as they drifted by George Washington's home, the troops grinned and saluted. By sunset they laid anchor just beyond the reach of the guns of Fort Washington.

As the ships' gunners began to pepper the fort in preparation for a landing, a sudden explosion rent the air. There could be no mistaking the sound. The soldiers at Fort Washington had blown up their own powder magazine and were now in full retreat. A British landing party was immediately dispatched and reported that the fort was incapacitated, the guns spiked, the buildings destroyed. Now that the fort was no longer a threat, Gordon was free to return to the main fleet. His mission was done. But the daring officer was not yet done with the Americans. He ordered the ships on to Alexandria, Virginia, where the citizens promptly surrendered to him. Thrilled to be spared the fate that had befallen Washington, the citizens of Alexandria agreed to meet Gordon's terms and he soon departed down the Potomac with a wealth of goods and monies.

But not everyone was willing to accept Gordon's easy victory. Three American naval officers, including Oliver Hazard Perry, had been busily laying traps for Gordon all along the river. As the ships sailed slowly past, gunners fired at them from both sides while fireships appeared out of nowhere, determined to light the British ships ablaze. Perry was undaunted. He zigzagged through the American traps, even landing at one point to take out one rather persistent battery. Gordon's daring attack and his equally daring escape became the stuff of legends.

Cockburn's next target was a more personal one. He took a small group of sailors to the offices of the *National Intelligencer*, a newspaper whose editor, Joseph Galestone, had been one of the most critical of Cockburn's actions in the Chesapeake. There he ordered the presses smashed and had all the type cases dumped into the street, telling his men to ensure that "all the C's are destroyed so that he cannot abuse my name anymore."[8] But when Cockburn announced his intention to burn the building down several neighbour women pleaded with him not to, afraid that their own nearby homes would catch fire as well.

Though Cockburn cheerfully burned all of the public buildings in Washington, he was adamant that private property be respected and ordered several of his men flogged for looting private homes. He was especially furious when a prostitute was brought to him claiming she had been shot by one of his soldiers. He announced that the man responsible would be executed but the woman could not identify the solider. Instead, Cockburn offered her a handful of gold coins. Less than 24 hours after he first entered Washington, Cockburn finally began to make his preparations to leave the city. After ordering a dusk-to-dawn curfew, he and his men quietly slipped away. On his way back to his ships Cockburn again encountered the wounded Barney, still in the company of Cockburn's man. The American agreed to see that the British dead were properly buried.

After the raid on Washington, Cockburn returned to harrying the Chesapeake coast until the close of the war. He participated in the ill-fated raid on New Orleans and when word of the Treaty of Ghent finally reached the coast, he adamantly refused to return any of the escaped slaves who had sought refuge in his camps as the treaty terms decreed. After the war Cockburn continued his illustrious career, rising to the rank of admiral of the fleet, serving as the lead escort when Napoleon Bonaparte was taken to St. Helens, and then serving as governor of that island. But he considered his work for Canada, particularly the raid on Washington, his greatest achievement.

CHAPTER TEN:
THE LORDS OF THE SEA

"The madness which for many years has pervaded the European continent has at length reached this Hemisphere."[1]

This line from *Nova Scotia Royal Gazette* is typical of how Maritimers greeted the
news that the Americans had declared war. Like most Canadians, the residents of the
Maritime colonies did not embrace the idea of war. They thought the war threatened the lucrative seaborne trade they enjoyed with their U.S. neighbours. Instead,
the war would eventually provide an economic windfall to the entire east coast.

Trade continued between the eastern British colonies and the eastern seaboard of the United States, despite the fact that battles were raging at the other
end of the St. Lawrence. Special licences were given to allow American cargo
ships access to the port of Halifax, and when the war became especially heated the
Americans would "arrange" to have the ships seized by the British and then make
a quiet but healthy profit on their cargo while they appeared to be "ransoming"
their boats. Authorities turned a blind eye, and with a good reason. American
goods bought at Halifax made their way across the Pacific to supply the British
troops fighting Napoleon or were loaded onto ships and sent down the St. Lawrence River for the use of British and Canadian soldiers fighting the Americans in
Upper Canada. In fact, many of these New England goods would end up as supplies on the very British ships that were engaged in blockading the United States
east coast! A busy trade developed in the other direction as well. The U.S. craved
the goods that British ships brought from Europe.

For their part, many of the Americans along the coast were slow to embrace a
war by which they had much to lose and little to gain. Maine declared that it

would "not molest their Neighbours the Inhabitants of New Brunswick." This trade — both legal and illicit — established Halifax as the major eastern-Canadian port through which goods bound for England and for Upper Canada would pass. It also greatly elevated the colony's wealth and kept a steady stream of goods and supplies moving toward the British Army. But there was another, less tangible, effect that was immediately recognized by the governor of Nova Scotia, Sir John Coape Sherbrooke. By continuing to trade with the Americans, they were undermining the American war effort and circumventing any hostile American attention by diverting them to trade and profit. But American and British cargo ships were not the only boats frequenting Halifax Harbour. There were others who trolled the deep waters off the eastern shoals, seeking much richer prizes — privateers. By the end of the war nearly 50 vessels carried royal Letters of Marque: licences issued by the crown allowing a ship to search, seize, and even destroy enemy ships, cargo, and personnel. They could also keep any spoils, but they had to be shared with the licence issuer.

Status Quo

A string of American victories encouraged Britain to sue for an end to the war in Canada. But despite the victories, the Americans lacked the political power to force unfavourable terms on the British. Thus, when negotiators sat down to hammer out the terms of the Treaty of Ghent, neither side had a real advantage.

The treaty took nearly one month to cross the Atlantic. When it finally arrived, its terms shocked many of those who had fought on both sides. Hostilities would end, property and prisoners would be returned, and a joint commission would be struck to look at boundary problems. Essentially, everything returned to what it had been when the war began. Even more significantly, neither impressments nor embargoes, the reasons given for the invasion of Canada, were even mentioned in the treaty!

CANADA ON FIRE

The war was a mere whisper when Enos Collins, a wily and determined Nova Scotia entrepreneur, took a stroll along the Halifax docks to view a collection of captured ships that were to be put up for auction. One in particular caught his eye, though it was hard to imagine why. The ship was a tiny, dilapidated Spanish slaver with little to recommend it beyond the fact that it still lay above the waterline. A closer look would have brought Mr. Collins nearer to the rotting stench of its previous human cargo that even then seemed to seep through the slats of its hold. She was called the *Black Joke* for good reason. There seemed little of value left in the ship.

But Enos Collins frequently saw opportunity where others saw only difficulty. He was the second son of a prominent Nova Scotian with little formal education and virtually no prospects. He went to sea at a very young age as a cabin boy and quickly made his way through the ranks until he became a captain. Collins soon realized that the real money to be made at sea lay in owning, not working on, privateers. He bought interests in several ships. It was said that when Collins had heard that the British Peninsular Army was blockaded by the Spaniards at Cadiz, Spain, and suffering from a lack of provisions, he immediately loaded three ships with supplies and ordered that they boldly sail right through the blockade. The story made Collins a legend in Nova Scotia. The goods he carried were sold for a healthy profit to the desperate British Army, making him a very rich man.

Collins could see another opportunity in the *Black Joke*, and in the prospect of another war. He bought the ship and immediately had her scrubbed, repaired, and renamed the *Liverpool Packet*. Initially, the *Packet* ran mail and passengers between Liverpool, Nova Scotia, and Halifax. The scheme seemed to lack the usual boldness of a Collins endeavour, and the people of Liverpool wondered what he was really up to.

In June 1812, two weeks after the U.S. had declared war, a British schooner limped into Liverpool Harbour, its sails shredded by buckshot and its deck littered with wounded and dead. Its captain announced that his ship had barely escaped capture by an American frigate. This was exactly what Collins had been waiting for. The war had begun. The *Packet* was rushed back to harbour and fitted with five rusty cannons that had previously seen service as gateposts on a waterfront road. The guns were too big for the ship, most ships that size had fewer and much smaller guns, but those guns would come in very handy in the next few months. The *Packet*'s captain recruited an oversize-crew to man the ship. By mid-August she had her Letter of Marque. A few weeks later, the *Liverpool Packet* sailed out of port with Captain John Freeman at her helm.

The first prize in the war had been taken by another privateer a few days before, but the *Liverpool Packet* took up the challenge. She was out on the water for less than a week before she encountered the American merchant ship *Middlesex*. The men of the *Packet* quickly overcame the ship, set a small crew aboard her, and sent her to the vice admiralty court (also called a prize court) in Halifax, which would sell off the cargo and ship, and divvy up the profits between the various partners and the government. The next day, the *Liverpool Packet* picked up a second prize, a cargo ship that was at least four times her size. Unfortunately, a British Navy ship had already relieved this ship of her cargo of port wine destined for Rhode Island, but there remained enough for the entire *Packet* crew to a enjoy a celebration.

By the time the *Liverpool Packet* returned to port, another man was at its helm. Joseph Barss was barely 36 but he was an experience privateer and the brother of one of Collins's partners in the *Liverpool Packet*. No record exists of why Barss took over command, but it may have had something to do with drunken revelry overcoming the search for prizes. The son of a captain, Barss followed his father to the sea as soon as he was old enough. During the French wars, he served as an officer and then as a captain of several privateer vessels. He'd done well and had his share of adventures. When he was offered a place on the *Liverpool Packet* he saw the same potential that Collins did. The ship might have appeared too small and dilapidated to be of any use, but Barss also saw its sleek lines and knew it would be fast and easy to handle. And like Collins, Barss had heard the rumours and took note of the activity on the far shore. Something would happen, and soon. A wounded British schooner limping into port brought him just the news he was looking for.

Barss believed there were greater riches to be had by prowling the waters off Cape Cod and that is where he headed with the *Liverpool Packet*. Barss had several advantages. Along with a sleek, fast ship that could dart in quickly to capture a prize and duck the American naval vessels lying in wait to catch him, Barss had also developed a network that provided him with information about the location and route of most of the major ships leaving Cape Cod. At the centre of his network was his brother, John Barss, a Halifax merchant and assemblyman with extensive contacts all over the coast. Within weeks, Barss and his crew were wreaking havoc all over Massachusetts Bay and demonstrating an uncanny ability to locate and capture the most heavily laden cargo ships. In one week alone, the tiny privateer took 11 ships, putting

THE LORDS OF THE SEA

prize crews aboard each one and sending them back to Halifax to the prize court. Each captured ship required a skeleton crew to man her and eventually, even with extra men aboard, the *Liverpool Packet*'s incredible successes forced her to return to port to replenish her crew. But Barss spent little time savouring his success. In his next major haul, he took nine fishing vessels with over $50,000 worth of cargo.

Impatient and devastatingly successful, Barss began to send only the richest of his captures back to Halifax. After taking what he needed from the others, he released them in order to preserve his crew and focus his energies on the prizes that could bring him the best returns. With his successes along the American coast, Barss's exploits had become the stuff of legend. He was rumoured to be ruthless and impossible to best. Over 200 American vessels had fallen to him and his crew. The rumours grew wilder and the residents of the coast demanded that the U.S. government do something to stop the Canadian pirate who prowled their waters. With the American newspapers filled with exaggerated stories about his exploits and editorials calling for his capture, Barss spent the Christmas holidays at home enjoying his newfound wealth. The *Liverpool Packet* floated in Halifax Harbour, surrounded by no less than 21 of its prizes. In less than four months the *Liverpool Packet* had accumulated over $100,000 worth of prizes, which today would be worth more than $3 million. That was just the beginning. They would take dozens of more ships over the winter.

The papers were clamouring for action. Some suggested the creation of an inland canal across Cape Cod that would allow New England merchants to avoid the *Packet*, which lay in wait just outside the bay. Merchants began to recruit crews of seaman and outfit them for the express purpose of tracking down and capturing Barss and his ship.

In June 1813, the American privateer *Thomas* caught sight of the *Liverpool Packet* just off the coast of Maine. The Americans immediately set a course for the infamous Canadian privateer. Barss knew he was in trouble. The American ship was larger and more heavily gunned. Worse, she probably carried far more men. Barss had recently sent home several prize crews and he was running with a skeleton crew of 36. He decided to make a run for it. Barss took the helm and ordered the men to toss most of the heavy guns into the ocean in order to lighten the ship. The biggest gun he had moved to the stern, where he had his men keep up a steady stream of fire toward the pursuing *Thomas*. The chase continued for six hours before Barss finally struck his colours.

By then the Americans were incensed. They boarded the *Liverpool Packet* with muskets drawn and a fierce fight ensued. Several sailors were killed before the captains were able to call a halt. Despite the violence, Barss knew he had little to worry about. Privateer crews were routinely paroled and sent back to their home ports on a promise not to fight again. Unfortunately for the crew of the *Liverpool Packet*, the Americans did not consider this a routine capture. The Canadian crew had humiliated the Americans time and time again and vengeance was more important to the people of Portsmouth than any unwritten rules of engagement. Joseph Barss and his crew were shackled and paraded through the streets of Portsmouth while the citizens took the opportunity to heckle and humiliate them. The American captain was greeted as a hero.

The rough treatment did not end on the streets of Portsmouth. Barss and his crew were thrown into the town jail. Although captains could traditionally expect better treatment, Barss was offered the reverse. He was kept in fetters and fed only hardtack and water. He spent months in jail before the Americans finally agreed to his parole. Even then, they added extra terms. Before they would agree to let him go, Barss had to agree to give up his privateering against the Americans forever. Once he was finally back home in Liverpool, Nova Scotia, Barss kept the terms of his parole. His privateering days were done. Barss spent the rest of the war as captain of a series of merchant ships. One of the ships he commanded in the West Indies was the *Wolverine*, a ship captured from the Americans that he had once known as the *Thomas*. The Americans captured and imprisoned him again while he captained the *Wolverine*.

After the war, Barss bought a farm near Kemptville, Nova Scotia, and raised a large family with his wife. He would not get to enjoy his family or the wealth he had gained in the war for long. Barss died at the relatively young age of 48, perhaps as a result of his months spent in American prisons.

After the capture of the *Packet*, the vengeful residents of Portsmouth had wanted to torch the ship. But the authorities recognized its value, so she was repaired and christened *Young Teazer's Ghost* after another ship, *Young Teazer*, whose captain had set her ablaze rather than see her captured by the British. She was floated as an American privateer but after one voyage was sold and renamed the *Portsmouth Packet*. But the change in name did not change the ship's luck. The Canadians easily tracked the movements of the *Packet*, regularly reporting her location to merchants, privateers, and the British Navy. Finally, in October 1813, the British ship HMS *Fantome* captured the *Portsmouth Packet* and returned her once again to Canadian hands.

In Halifax Harbour, the *Packet* found some old friends. Enos Collins and his partners bought the ship again, for the same price they had purchased her for before. They put her to sea once more, this time with Barss's second-in-command, Caleb Seely, as her captain. Seely was an experienced privateer and the son of United Empire Loyalists who had fled the U.S. during the War of Independence. When the war began he took a job captaining a privateer named the *Star* out of Saint John, New Brunswick. But the governor of New Brunswick saw more potential in the illicit trade that had been established between the Americans and his colony, and eventually he refused to grant any more Letters of Marque. Although Seely's profits had been good, they were nothing like the *Liverpool Packet* could boast and the New Brunswicker eventually arrived in Liverpool to seek his share of that fortune. He would quickly find it with the *Packet*.

In 1813, Seely was granted a Letter of Marque from the governor of Nova Scotia that provided him with extensive permissions to "to apprehend, seize, and take the Ships, Vessels and Goods Belonging to the United States of America, or to any persons being Subjects of France."[2] Though Seely did not have the same success as Barss, his captures made him and his partners very wealthy. By the time he returned from his first run, he had already sent three sloops to the prize courts. Over the next nine months he sent an additional 14 American ships back to Liverpool with prize crews aboard. Though irritated with his success, the American papers wrote frequently of his humane and respectful treatment of American sailors he took prisoner. The prizes he deemed unworthy to send back were released intact and allowed to continue to their destination.

As a partner in the *Liverpool Packet*, Seely was able to keep a sizable amount of the profits earned by his ship. In the fall of 1814 he quit his life on the sea and prepared to marry Enos Collins's sister. Seely launched a lucrative export business dealing in fish, seal skin, and fur, and both he and Collins would frequently accompany their goods across the Atlantic. After the war ended, Seely became a judge and ran, unsuccessfully, for the legislative assembly.

During the war it was said that the *Packet* crews boarded from 150 to 200 American ships and sent 50 of the best prizes back to Liverpool. On December 4, 1814, the 50th prize captured by the *Liverpool Packet* was recorded in the prize courts. Then the most notorious ship on the eastern seaboard faded into oblivion. No mention is made of her again.

— — — —

While the *Liverpool Packet* was the most successful privateer, she was not the only Canadian privateer plying the waters along the American coast. The *Sir John Sherbrooke* was by far the largest of the privateers to sail out of the port of Halifax and its cache of prizes was worthy of its size. She was a ship made for privateering, with numerous heavy guns and rows of boarding pikes and cutlasses lining her upper decks. Her captain was a man who believed in iron discipline and a strict adherence to tradition. Joseph Freeman was a colonel in the local militia who'd distinguished himself fighting in the French wars. He was also a long-time privateer and a merchant who needed every ounce of the discipline he'd developed in the militia to keep his motley crew of foreigners and sailors-of-fortune under control. Every morning when the *Packet* was at sea he would order the 50 marines and 100 sailors and gunners who sailed with him to assemble on deck. He would read them the articles of war while the Red Jack fluttered in the wind high above him.

Freeman was also a wily privateer. After capturing one American brig with a rich cargo of sugar and coffee in its hold, he ordered his prize crew to continue flying the American colours. If they were stopped by the British they would supply their prize papers. In this way, they could sail unmolested back to Halifax. Within four months, the *Sir John Sherbrooke* brought home over 14 prizes and earned its owners over $50,000.

Unfortunately, the massive ship required extensive support to keep it running. Eventually, despite the prizes she brought home, the *Sir John Sherbrooke* was deemed too expensive to maintain as a privateer and she was put out as a merchant ship. That made her a prime target for American privateers, and in 1814 she was caught by the American privateer *Syren*. After the capture, the Americans tried to break through the tight British blockade. When it became clear that they were cornered, they burned the *Sherbrooke* rather than return her to Canadian hands. A few days later, the *Syren* was herself destroyed.

Joseph Freeman's younger brother, Thomas, had served as a prize master for the *Liverpool Packet*, sailing her prizes back to Liverpool Harbour. His earnings from that ship made him a wealthy man and he soon bought his own ship, the *Retaliation*. The *Retaliation* took home four prizes, earning young Freeman enough to finance his retirement. He took his winnings and settled in Nova Scotia. The *Retaliation* would continue to sail, bringing home numerous prizes to enrich its crew and owners.

The smallest privateering vessel to sail from Halifax was also its most interesting. The *Crown* was barely 40-feet-long. Captained by Solomon Jennings she squeezed in 30 crew members, most of whom were boys under the age of 16. The ship was so small that its young crew slept on deck, under the sail, and even the smallest boy could not go below deck without bumping his head. She carried a nine-pound cannon that made the entire ship shake whenever it was fired. But whatever she lacked in stature, stability, and size, the *Crown* more than made up for in heart. Only two days out of Halifax Harbour on her first privateering mission, her captain caught sight of a ship more than five times her size and immediately gave chase. The ship was an American brig named *Sibae* and she carried a rich cargo of cotton. Two hours after the chase started it ended with the *Crown*'s prize crew taking the helm. Unfortunately for the *Crown* and its crew, a British ship appeared and claimed they had been chasing the *Sibae*, earning them the right to claim joint capture. The Canadian crew protested loudly but only succeeded in annoying the British captain so much that he impressed two of them into the British Navy on the spot. That was a huge mistake on the part of the British, who had a lot to gain from respecting their privateer partners.

The *Crown* returned to port to drop off the prisoners from the *Sibae*. Several crew members defected, fearing they might be impressed into the British Navy if they risked another run. Still, the *Crown* sailed out again, its 19 remaining crew members determined to win more prizes. She captured several ships off the coast of Maine before her luck ran out. In April 1813, Jennings sighted the American schooner *Bream* and gave chase. It was a trap. The *Bream* swung around and turned her big guns on the tiny *Crown*, ripping massive holes in her mast and riggings.

Relations between privateers, merchants, and navies were not always so courteous. The privateer war had a dark side. Men on both sides were frequently killed in fierce firefights and hand-to-hand combat as ships were captured and recaptured. Just before the war began, a young sailor, William Paul, was killed in a violent engagement between an American privateer and a Canadian privateer, the Swallow. Left with two young children to support, Paul's wife, Almira, was devastated and blamed the Americans for her husband's death. "I conceived them alone the authors of my misery, and regretted that my sex prevented my placing myself in a situation in which I might have been enabled to avenge his death,"[25] she wrote in her journal. With no friends to lend her support and a growing desire for revenge, Almira did not let the fact that she was a woman hold her back for long.

As Major-General Isaac Brock was finalizing his plans for Canada's defence and hurrying toward Amherstburg, Almira Paul finally found a way to make money and avenge her husband's death. After cutting her hair and donning some of her husband's old clothes, she packed up her children and took them to her mother's home. Then she made her way down to the wharf. Hundreds of people scurried over the long wooden docks — sailors returning from leave, merchants selling their wares, wives and daughters watching for a loved one's return. More people moved in and out of the low wooden buildings skirting the docks. Inside, representatives of the privateers and navy ships were signing on new men to replace those who had taken their winnings and gone home and those who had died while seeking their fortune. Almira entered one of the buildings and signed on, under the name of Jack Brown, as a cook's helper aboard the Dolphin. *A few days later, Almira, wearing a tightly bound undergarment under her husband's clothes to hide her figure, was enduring her first battle at sea — and a devastating bout of seasickness. Just as she found her sea legs, she witnessed the capture of the British frigate* Guerrière *by the American privateer* Constitution, *an event that caused her to "despair of very soon meeting with an opportunity to revenge the death of my husband."[4]*

As Almira watched in horror, the Guerrière *and* Constitution *collided and became entangled, with the* Constitution *constantly firing broadsides at the British ship. The British shot seemed to bounce harmlessly off the American ship's sides. When the two ships finally managed to pull apart, the force caused the* Guerrière's *mast to collapse and the captain surrendered. The ship had been so badly damaged that the American captain ordered it burned. The* Dolphin, *too far away to assist, quickly sailed away to safety. Almira continued her adventures, participating in sea battles and serving on three ships. She was wounded once and captured twice, she escaped both times. She encountered some of the worst cruelties of shipboard life, including beatings by a "vile, malicious and inhuman" chief cook. When she took the opportunity to kick the cruel cook overboard, she watched in dismay as other crew members plucked him from a shark-infested sea. She confessed her deed and was flogged in front of the entire ship's crew, her only solace was that tradition dictated that she wear a shirt during the flogging and she was able to keep her secret. She stayed at sea for three years, travelling from the American coast to the Strait of Gibraltar without anyone suspecting she was a woman. When she finally returned home she was "pleased to think to what length a female might carry her adventures, what hardships she could endure and what dangers brave."[5] In 1816, a book was published based on her adventures.*

Captain Jennings would later write that the musket balls tore holes in the shirts and hats of his men, but he cheerfully related that not a man or boy was killed or wounded on either side. After putting up a valiant fight, Jennings finally struck his colours, and he and his crew surrendered. The Americans were very impressed with the young crew of the *Crown* and treated them as minor celebrities during their imprisonment, before arranging their parole and return to Halifax at the earliest opportunity.

———— ——— ————

If there is any debate about who won the War of 1812, there can certainly be no doubt as to who won the war on the eastern seaboard. By the time the Treaty of Ghent was signed, troops from Nova Scotia occupied no less than half of the state of Maine. Canadians privateers had captured four times as many ships as their American counterparts and placed a stranglehold on American trade that saw American exports reduced from $45,000,000 before the war to less than $7,000,000 when it ended. And while the Canadian Maritime economies enjoyed unprecedented prosperity during and immediately after the war, the American economy suffered a deep recession from which they were very slow to recover.

Over the course of the war, 41 Canadian privateers ruled the waters between the Maritime colonies and states, taking literally hundreds of American ships as prizes. Nova Scotia, New Brunswick, and even Newfoundland thrived on the profits brought in by those ships. Enos Collins, who had seen so much potential in a stinky, rundown former slaver, was touted as the richest man in North America by the close of the war.

CHAPTER ELEVEN:
THE MAN OF THE FUTURE

There are certain people who have the fortune, or occasionally the misfortune, to serve as witnesses to some of the most amazing events in human history. William Hamilton Merritt was just such a man. As a militiaman serving in his father's unit, and later at the head of his own elite troop of militia Dragoons, William was both a witness to — and participant in — most of the major battles of the War of 1812.

Like his father before him, William Merritt was fiercely loyal. His father had fought for the British in the American War of Independence and afterward moved to Canada as a United Empire Loyalist. William's loyalties belonged solely to Canada.

William Merritt was born in Twelve Mile Creek, a small community at the northern end of the Niagara Peninsula, about 20 kilometres west of Fort George and the American border. The Niagara Peninsula was home, and he would protect it fiercely.

By the age of 20, Merritt had already fought alongside Brock at Queenston, and with FitzGibbon at Stoney Creek and Beaver Dams. The young man had no illusions about war.

Living in a state of constant warfare was having a devastating effect on everyone in the region. On July 8, 1813, Merritt took part in a particularly violent skirmish between the Mohawks and Americans. Fighting alongside the Mohawks was a 13-year-old boy named John Lawe. His older brother had been killed in an earlier battle and his father had been wounded and taken prisoner. The boy's desire for revenge overwhelmed him. Long after the battle was officially over he was still stumbling around the field in a state of shock, searching for the enemy. Eventually, his mother came to find him and carried the exhausted lad home in her arms.

Merritt was disgusted with the British whenever they temporarily retreated from the Niagara Peninsula, as they so often did as their fortunes rose and fell during the war. He felt they were abandoning the settlers on the frontier, especially the Loyalists, who would pay the biggest price when the Americans swarmed over the border. Like FitzGibbon, Merritt was angry about the enemy's harassment of the civilians and swore to do something about it. Even during the periods when the militia had been disbanded, Merritt and his fellow Dragoons galloped around the countryside, harassing the enemy. They clashed frequently with the hated Cyrenius Chapin and his guerrillas. But as angry as Merritt was with the Americans, it was the actions of a fellow Canadian that appalled him the most.

Joseph Willcocks was a man with a grudge against the British. Although he had fought with Brock at Queenston, his allegiance shifted soon after. The Irish immigrant to Upper Canada hated the British and, by extension, anyone loyal to Britian. He was the publisher of the *Upper Canadian Guardian*, where he regularly attacked the British and Loyalists in print. Willcocks was twice jailed for libel. Unfortunately for the British and those loyal to them, Willcocks also had a seat in the legislature in the town of York.

In 1813, convinced that the Americans would win the war, Willcocks turned on the people he had been elected to represent. He started by passing on snippets of military intelligence. His actions were treasonous, but not really unusual at a time when loyalties were unpredictable on both sides of the border. But mere spying was not enough for Willcocks. He became a colonel in the American Army while still serving in the Upper Canadian legislature. He also managed to recruit more than 100 of his fellow Canadians to fight against the Canadians and the British.

In the fall of 1813, the Americans invaded the Niagara Peninsula again. By December, they had taken Fort George and were also in Queenston and Chippewa, just 25 kilometres east of Twelve Mile Creek. Willcocks took the opportunity to exact a little revenge on the Loyalist communities. He and his men rode around the countryside, looting and burning the farms of his former neighbours and constituents. He arrested prominent Loyalists and sent them to prisons in the

United States. In Twelve Mile Creek, Willcocks arrested an 80-year-old former town warden who was a retired militiaman — a man by the name of Thomas Merritt. Thomas was William Merritt's father.

The Americans took Thomas across the border but released him soon after. They left the elderly man to find his own way back home as best he could. When William Merritt heard of this, he was livid. In his journal, Merritt wrote that he had taken "many [a] long and weary ride, in the lonely hours of the night, in hope of catching Willcocks and making an example of him and all traitors."[1]

On November 28, 1813, Willcocks and his men were in the area of Twelve Mile Creek. Merritt was soon on their trail and slowly closing in on them. To his frustration, Willcocks slipped away. However, two of Willcocks's men happened upon Merritt and his crew and mistook them for Americans; the blue uniforms the Canadians wore were similar to those of some of the American regiments. From these two men, Merritt learned that the Americans, who were in possession of Fort George at that point, had left the fort and were heading for the British position at Burlington Heights. Apparently, Willcocks and his men were acting as scouts ahead of the main force.

Merritt chased after the traitor and a dangerous game of cat and mouse ensued. After several close calls, Willcocks escaped and returned to the main force to report to his American commander. Willcocks drastically inflated the size of the British force in the area. He reasoned that the Americans would give him more leeway to interrogate and arrest British sympathizers if they thought the British forces were a real threat. The Americans, thinking they could not run the British out of Burlington Heights after all, abandoned their foray and began marching back to Fort George.

Merritt and his commander, Colonel Murray, wanted to pursue the Americans. Both men believed they could defeat their enemies while they were outside the safety of the fort. Unfortunately, they were under strict orders not to follow the retreating Americans beyond Twelve Mile Creek. It was a bitter blow.

Merritt was also very worried about his father, who was still making his way home. He found out that Thomas had reached Shipman's Corners, a no man's land between the British and American positions. Merritt asked for permission to leave Twelve Mile Creek on the pretext of rounding up American spies. He then went directly to Shipman's Corners and took his father home to safety.

During his foray, he saw numerous American scouts. He thought they were probably trying to evaluate the strength of the forces in Twelve Mile Creek before deciding on their next move. As soon as he got back home he called up the militia and told them to assemble in the town centre. Every available man and boy answered the call. When the American scouts saw the huge crowd, they were convinced it was an advance party and that the entire British and Canadian force would soon follow. That, of course, was untrue. At that time, the British had no intention of advancing from their position at Burlington Heights. However, this deceptive show of force was enough to persuade the commander at Fort George, Brigadier General George McClure, that he should abandon the peninsula altogether.

McClure made plans to withdraw across the Niagara River to the relative safety of their own Fort Niagara. Willcocks was furious. He had cast his lot in with the enemy and believed an American victory was within easy reach.

The Americans decided to destroy Fort George to prevent it from falling into the hands of the British. Willcocks asked McClure for permission to burn the nearby town of Newark before they burned the fort. He argued that this would prevent the inhabitants from offering shelter or sustenance to British soldiers.

At dusk on December 10, 1813, Willcocks and his men, accompanied by a few American militiamen, rode into the town of Newark. The townspeople were warned to take what they could from their homes and leave. It had been snowing all day and it was bitterly cold. Willcocks started the fire at the home of an old political foe, a Loyalist by the name of William Dickson, who had already been arrested. Willcocks carried the firebrand himself. He went upstairs to find the elderly Mrs. Dickson in bed. She was too ill to walk, so he ordered two of his men to carry her outside. The men wrapped the old woman in blankets and set her in a snowdrift. She watched in anguish as Willcocks burned her home to the ground.

There were other, equally horrific stories from that night. One young widow with three small children was turned out of her home with nothing but a few coins. After Willcocks's men plundered and torched her home, they took her money as well. In all, 400 women, children, and elderly men were turned out into the snow that night.

On that day, Merritt had been on an assignment in Beaver Dams with Colonel Murray. As they were making their way back home, they saw the eerie orange glow of the fires in Newark. They guessed what had happened and raced to the scene, but they were already too late.

Of all the horrifying scenes Merritt had witnessed during the war, this was the worst. All that was left of Newark were glowing embers and charred buildings. Of the 150 homes in the town, only one remained standing. The townspeople had crowded into every room until the house could hold no more. Those left outside huddled in the snow drifts and beneath makeshift shelters. Some, terrified there might be more attacks, had stumbled off into the freezing night to seek shelter at outlying farms.

The streets were scattered with the remnants of a once prosperous town. Furniture, clothing, dishes, and personal treasures were everywhere, all abandoned by people too cold to carry them. The next morning, William and his men found the frozen bodies of the women and children who had been seeking shelter outside the town. They had lost their way in the blackness of the night. As many as 100 women and children had perished that night in Newark. Willcocks had certainly had his revenge. Soldiers and civilians were equally horrified at this atrocity. The burning of Newark, more than any other action in the war, united the Canadian and British troops with the civilians.

Merritt was enraged. And he was not the only one. The British and Canadian troops swore vengeance, and Colonel Murray was so furious that he ordered his troops to Fort George that very night, ignoring the direct orders of General Vincent not to advance. As the British and Canadian troops galloped toward the fort, most of the American troops, along with the traitor Willcocks, were already retreating across the border. Colonel Murray and his men captured the few remaining Americans who were still at Fort George and then secured the fort. Neither Murray nor William was ever chastised for disobeying orders that night — the horror of Newark was too great.

Ten days later, on December 20, 1813, the reprisals began. Merritt and his Dragoons had commandeered anything that could float. They were preparing to follow the Americans across the icy river and attack them at Fort Niagara. It had taken the Dragoons several long days and nights of toiling in the bitter cold to secure all the boats. On the night of the attack, exhausted and gripped by fever, William collapsed. He was not able to participate in the invasion he had so wanted to be part of. It was another blow for the young man.

The American fort was heavily defended and no easy target, but it faltered quickly under the vengeful Canadian and British assault. The officers had a difficult time controlling their soldiers' bloodlust, and more than one American soldier lost his life in a private battle to avenge those lost at Newark.

Within days, the American side of the Niagara, from Fort Niagara to Buffalo, New York, was a charred ruin. In the town of Buffalo only three buildings were left standing when the raid was over. There were atrocities committed by the Canadians and British in those battles, too. American families lost their homes and possessions. Some lost their lives to Native tomahawks. No one, it seemed, felt the need to curb the warriors' desire for vengeance anymore. The war had taken a very ugly turn.

The Americans did not blame the British, the Canadians, or even the Native warriors. They held their own man, George McClure, responsible. He had allowed the burning of Newark and fuelled the spate of vengeful attacks. He was taunted and threatened on the streets of Buffalo and was soon relieved of his command.

Finally, after the many horrors during the winter of 1813, it was too cold to fight any longer. The desire for vengeance had, at long last, been exhausted. The British and Canadian soldiers retreated to their side of the Niagara River to wait for the spring thaw.

The next move came from the Americans. On July 3, 1814, in sore need of a victory and with their border in ruins, the Americans captured Fort Erie at the southern end of the Niagara Peninsula. Then they marched toward Fort Chippewa, 10 kilometres to the north, reaching it the next day. While the troops were marching, William Merritt was having a celebratory dinner with his parents at

Twelve Mile Creek. He had just turned 21. However, as soon as he heard the news, Merritt dashed off to join the other reinforcements racing to join the battle.

Next day, July 5, the British commander at Fort Chippewa, Major-General Phineas Riall, watched the Americans approach. The American soldiers were wearing grey uniforms, making Riall think he was facing a unit of raw militia recruits. He confidently ordered a full-frontal assault, believing the militia would turn tail and run. But the soldiers did not run. Riall and his men were actually facing an entire army of hardened, well-trained career soldiers. Apparently, the Americans had run out of the blue wool used to make uniforms for the regular troops, so they had used the grey instead.

Near the close of battle, while his men were in retreat, Riall desperately charged at the Americans with only his aide at his side. He turned back only when the aide was wounded. By the time the reinforcements arrived, the battle was already over.

The British retreated to the village, where their cannons were in place. The Americans could see it would be difficult to breach that defence, so they decided not to pursue the remnants of Riall's army. That night, the houses of Chippewa were filled with wounded and dying soldiers. It was a night the villagers would never forget. Neither the British nor the Canadians were willing to give up the field yet. The British withdrew to Fort George, while the Americans camped on Queenston Heights and waited for reinforcements to arrive by ship. However, the commander of the reinforcements was sick with fever and refused to let his ships sail without him. The Americans at Queenston continued to wait, becoming increasingly restless.

William Merritt spent most of the next month skirmishing with the Americans. The Niagara Peninsula was once again under siege and the civilians suffered for it. Willcocks and his band of traitors were riding again. They raided village after village, plundering and forcing the population to flee to the safety of the British forts.

But Willcocks's men were not the only ones raiding. A small group of the American soldiers still cooped up at Queenston Heights needed an outlet for their frustration. They rode to the village of St. David's and easily drove back the few

British soldiers guarding the villagers. The Americans looted and burned the town. By the time William and his men arrived to help relieve the beleaguered British soldiers, 40 homes had already been destroyed. Nothing could be done to undo the wrong, but the American commanders made some amends by disciplining the soldiers responsible for the destruction. The soldiers were reprimanded and immediately dismissed from service.

On July 23, 1814, the Americans received word that the reinforcements they had been waiting for would not be coming. The British and Canadians, on the other hand, had been getting more reinforcements almost daily. The next day, the American commander retreated to Chippewa in order to re-supply his troops. From there, he planned to attack Burlington Heights. In the meantime, the British and Canadians had mobilized. They marched to Lundy's Lane, where Riall had sent William, along with several other officers, to scout the American positions.

On July 25, the American commander sent out a brigade of 1,200 men to search the same area for enemy troops. The brigade was led by Colonel Winfield Scott, an impetuous young man. On that same day, while searching the countryside, William and his men stopped for refreshments at a tavern owned by a widow named Deborah Wilson. The widow Wilson was well-known to both armies. She indiscriminately dished out both liquor and information to the patrons seated at her wooden tables, be they British, Canadian, or American.

William and his men were just about to sit down when a scout rushed in to tell them the Americans were on their way. The Canadians raced outside and jumped on their horses. As the American brigade approached, they began firing. William paused for a second and cheekily waved to them before galloping off.

Scott searched the tavern, but no soldiers were found. Then he questioned the Widow Wilson. She quickly told Scott what William had told her: Major-General Riall was waiting at a nearby farm with 1,100 men. She was right; Riall was nearby, but he was accompanied by almost three times that many soldiers.

Scott was anxious to fight and did not want to wait for reinforcements. Instead, he blindly rushed in to engage the enemy. He had 1,200 men, so he reasoned that 1,100 men would not prove to be a problem.

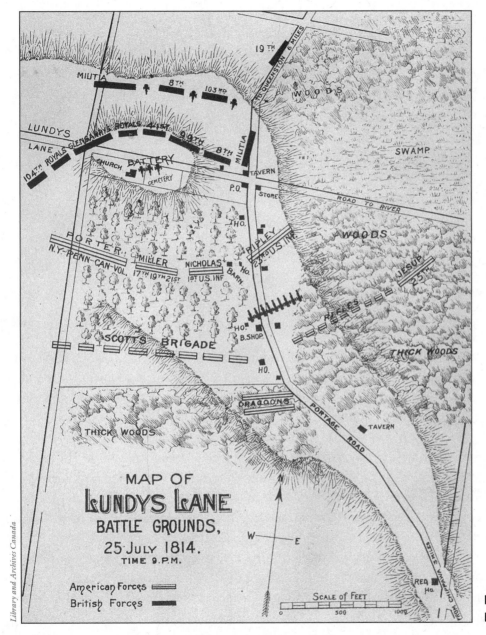

MAP OF
LUNDYS LANE
BATTLE GROUNDS,
25 JULY 1814.
TIME 9.P.M.

American Forces
British Forces

SCALE OF FEET
0   500   1000

Map of the Lundy's
Lane battleground.

The Battle of Lundy's Lane.

The battle raged all afternoon and into the night. The two armies were often only metres apart. They could easily see the faces of their enemies. Yet still they fought on, firing volley after volley. One soldier wrote that the battle was fought with a desperation verging on madness.

Willcocks was in the battle. He was afraid of being captured, for he knew he would be hanged as a traitor. The Upper Canadian government had already tried and found him guilty in absentia. Around midnight, fearing the battle would be lost, he disappeared into the darkness. In the blackness of night, horrific mistakes were made. Troops fired on themselves. Men engaged in hand-to-hand combat only to discover that the man they grappled with was one of their own. At one point, a group of American soldiers fought their way through the woods and surrounded Riall. He was taken prisoner, but his men fought on. Merritt, who had joined the battle as soon as the firing had started, attempted a rescue. But he was captured as well.

The Battle of Lundy's Lane, by C.W. Jefferys.

By morning, the men of both sides were too exhausted to continue. The battle was finally over. The Americans had quit the field, leaving their wounded and heavy artillery behind in their haste. The British were in no condition to follow the retreating Americans. The battlefield was littered with hundreds of bodies. Those who were there said it was difficult to distinguish the casualties from those who had merely fallen into an exhausted sleep. It took all morning to separate the wounded from the dead. The British and Canadian dead were buried in a mass

THE MAN OF THE FUTURE

grave, and the American dead were burnt in a giant funeral pyre.

In their hasty retreat back to Fort Erie, the Americans were forced to dump wagonloads of supplies and arms in order to use their wagons to transport the wounded. William Merritt was an unwilling participant in that retreat. The Americans took him and their other prisoners to jails in the United States.

Lundy's Lane was one of the bloodiest battles of the war. The British and Canadians suffered 880 men wounded, captured, or killed. The Americans suffered a similar number of casualties. Both sides claimed victory. Although the Americans had abandoned the field, the battle did a lot to prop up the flagging American enthusiasm for the war.

The horrors of that day were recorded by a young British surgeon named William "Tiger" Dunlop. As the only surgeon on the battlefield he had to tend 220 wounded men. In his journal he recounted the story of one woman who entered the makeshift surgery. She was searching for her elderly husband. When she finally found him, she saw that he had been mortally wounded. The woman sank down beside her husband and cried. Then, momentarily stunned by the devastation surrounding her, she took her dying husband's head on her lap and cried out, "O that the King and the President were both here this moment to see the misery their quarrels lead to — they surely would never go to war without a cause that they could give as a reason to God at the last day, for thus destroying the creatures that He had made in his own image?"[2]

— — — —

Whimpers of War

At the end of July, the Americans entrenched in Fort Erie were preparing for yet another invasion. But their plans were interrupted. On August 15, 1814, the British attacked the fort. The British and Canadians won a decisive victory and finally drove the Americans back across the border. William Merritt's friends and family at Twelve Mile Creek, and the other Niagara villagers, had endured their

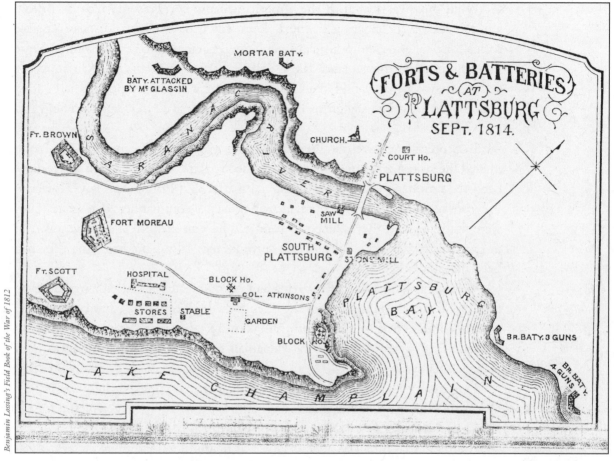

Forts and batteries at Plattsburgh.

last battle. They had also endured their last torment from Joseph Willcocks. The hated traitor was killed in the battle. Merritt, who was imprisoned in the United States, cheered when he heard the news.

On August 25, 1814, the Canadians and British swarmed into the naval base at Bladensburg, New York, one of the entry points to Washington, and easily disarmed the militia guarding the base. By nightfall, the Capitol itself had been set afire. Public buildings were looted and documents littered the city streets.

THE MAN OF THE FUTURE

While fire was ravaging the American capital, representatives of Britain and America were meeting in the Belgian town of Ghent to discuss possible terms for peace. As the politicians continued their negotiations, soldiers were fighting more battles on land, lakes, and sea. The Canadians and British won a series of naval victories on Lake Champlain. The war with Napoleon had ended and 16,000 battle-hardened troops had recently arrived in Canada to help end the war.

In September, Governor Prevost began a march on Plattsburgh, New York. He led the largest army the British had fielded to date. His land attack was to have occurred simultaneously with a British naval attack on Plattsburgh Bay. However, Prevost was in a hurry. He put pressure on the naval commanders to engage. They were not ready, but they reluctantly followed his commands. The battle was over in just over two hours — the British surrendered. It was the first time they had been defeated at sea.

When Prevost heard that the navy had been defeated he called a retreat, even though his troops outnumbered the enemy three to one. His commanders were devastated and tried to argue with him, but he refused to listen. The army retreated. They were halfway to the Canadian border before the Americans even realized they were gone.

On January 8, 1815, British and Canadian troops attacked the port of New Orleans, Louisiana. The Americans won a stunning victory there. The toll for the British and Americans was 2,000 dead or wounded.

In other circumstances, a victory of that magnitude might have won the war for the Americans. In fact, for a few weeks after the battle, the American populace believed the war was theirs. But it had all been for naught. Two weeks before the battle in New Orleans, on December 24, 1814, the negotiators in Ghent had signed a treaty officially ending the war.

When word of the peace finally reached North America in February 1815, William Merritt was at last allowed to go back home to Twelve Mile Creek. He married and raised a family in the little town he loved. An enterprising man, he was one of the visionaries who proposed the creation of the Welland Canal just a

The Battle of New Orleans

As the Treaty of Ghent was making its ponderous way across the Atlantic via a naval warship, the two massive armies were lining up near the city of New Orleans, Louisiana. The British/Canadian force was the larger of the two — some 7,500 regulars and militia. The American force, though smaller at 5,000 regulars and militia, was no less formidable.

The battle began at the end of December and had raged for nearly a month in various locations across Louisiana and at sea, as the British Navy engaged the fledgling American Navy. But no decisive blow was landed by either side. Finally the Americans dug in just outside New Orleans using deep trenches and hay bales as a buttress against the onslaught of the British guns. In front of the Americans lay a wide-open field that the British would be forced to cross in order to reach the American line.

Under cover of a dense fog, at 5:00 a.m. on January 8, 1815, the British commander sounded the advance. The British regulars and Canadian militia slowly picked their way across the open field with the fog covering their movements. But just as they neared the American line, the fog suddenly lifted, exposing the soldiers to American artillery fire.

George Gleig, a young British soldier, described the carnage that followed,

> *The shrieks of the wounded, therefore, the crash of firelocks, and the fall of such as were killed, caused at first some little confusion; and what added to the panic, was, that from the houses beside which we stood bright flames suddenly burst out. The Americans, expecting this attack, had filled them with combustibles for the purpose; and directing against them one or two guns, loaded with red-hot shot, in an instant set them on fire. The scene was altogether very sublime. A tremendous cannonade mowed down our ranks, and deafened us with its roar; whilst two large chateaux and their*

out-buildings almost scorched us with the flames, and blinded us with the smoke which they emitted.

Over 2,000 British soldiers died on the field outside New Orleans. Barely one month later, the Treaty to end the war finally arrived. It had been signed on December 24.

few years after the end of the war. He also took part in convincing the American and Canadian governments to build a bridge across the Niagara River, the former border between the two countries.

NOTES

Chapter One: Brock the Bold

1. General Isaac Brock to his brother Irving Brock, Niagara, January 10, 1811.
2. Thomas Jefferson in a letter to William Duane, editor of the *Aurora*, quoted in Henry Stevens Randall, *The Life of Thomas Jefferson*, Volume 3 (California: Derby and Johnson, 1858), 357.
3. Carl Benn, *The War of 1812* (Toronto: Osprey Publishing Ltd., 2002), 27.
4. *Ibid.*
5. *Ibid.*
6. "Sir Isaac Brock," *Dictionary of Canadian Biography*, Volume 5 (Toronto: University of Toronto Press, 2000).
7. Tecumseh , quoted in Allan W. Eckert, *A Sorrow in Our Heart: The Life of Tecumseh* (Toronto: Bantam Books, 1993), 719.
8. Sir Isaac Brock, quoted in Ferdinand Brock Tupper, *The Life and Correspondence of Sir Isaac Brock* (London: Simpkin, Marshall and Co., 1857).
9. Quoted in Donald R. Hickey, *The War of 1812: A Forgotten Conflict* (Chicago: University of Illinois Press, 1989), 82.
10. Brock in a letter to his brothers, Lake Ontario, September 3, 1812.
11. Quoted in David Breakenridge Read, *The Life and Times of Major-General Sir Isaac Brock, K.B.* (University of California: W. Briggs, 1894), 219.
12. Jarvis Narrative, DHC, 4:146.
13. Thomas G. Rideout in a letter his brother George, Brown's Point, October 21, 1812.
14. Anne Ilbert , quoted in Walter R. Nursey, *The Story of Sir Isaac Brock* (Toronto: McClelland and Stewart, 1923), 213.

Chapter Two: The Voyageurs

1. Captain Charles Roberts in a letter to Major John B. Glegg, aide-de-camp to General Isaac Brock, Fort Michilimackinac. July 29, 1812.

2. "William MacKay," *Dictionary of Canadian Biography*, Volume 5 (Toronto: University of Toronto Press).

3. Also known as *mariage à la facon du pays*, marriages conducted in the *custom of the country* were conducted outside European law or Christian rite between fur traders and native women. The marriages brought the fur traders many advantages. Their wives were well able to withstand the rigours of frontier life and brought their husbands additional contacts and invaluable loyalty from their large extended families.

4. This Montreal-based club restricted its membership to wealthy fur merchants, retired traders, and partners, most from the North West Company. The Beaver Club formed the heart of Montreal society in the late 18th and early 19th centuries.

5. Robert Allen, *His Majesties Allies: British Indian Policy in the Defence of Canada, 1774–1775* (Toronto: Dundurn Press, 1996), 153.

6. Porter Hanks in a letter to General Hull following the surrender of Fort Michimilimackinac, quoted in Dwight H. Kelton, *Annals of Fort Mackinac* (Detroit: Detroit Free Press Printing Co., 1882), 54.

7. Ross Cox, quoted in Rene Chartrand and Gerry Embleton, *British Forces in North America, 1793–1815* (Toronto: Osprey Publishing, 1998), 24.

8. "William MacKay," *Dictionary of Canadian Biography*, Volume 5 (Toronto: University of Toronto Press).

Chapter Three: John Norton and the Ghost Warriors

1. Reverend John Strachan, quoted in Carl Benn, *The Iroquois in the War of 1812* (Toronto: University of Toronto Press, 1998), 46.

2. Gordon Drummond, quoted in *Report of the Public Archives of Canada*, (Ottawa, 1896).

Chapter Four: James FitzGibbon and the Bloody Boys

1. Billy Green, quoted in *Ontario History*, Vol. 29 (Toronto: Ontario Historical Society, 1952), 175.

2. Quoted in the Ontario Historical Society, *The Defended Border: Upper Canada and the War of 1812* (Toronto: Macmillan Canada, 1964), 313.

3. Captain James FitzGibbon in a letter to Captain William J. Kerr, York, March 30, 1818.

4. This is an oft-repeated adage is most frequently attributed to John Norton, the Mohawk Chief. Source: Notes by Captain W.H. Merritt, *The Documentary History of the Campaign upon the Niagara Frontier*, Part 2, Lieut-Col. E. Cruickshank, Ed. (The Lundy's Lane Historical Society, 1900), 123.

5. Quoted in "A Soldier of Fortune," *The New Yorker*, February 16, 1839, Vol. VI, No. 22.

6. Captain James FitzGibbon in a letter to Mr. Walter Mackenzie, Lower Ward, Windsor Castle, May 10, 1855.

Chapter Five: Tecumseh

1. Tecumseh in a speech to the Ossages in Missouri during the winter of 1811–12.

2. John B. Glegg, quoted in Allan W. Eckert, *A Sorrow in Our Heart: The Life of Tecumseh* (New York: Bantum, 1992), 950.

3. Tecumseh to William Henry Harrison, Governor of the Indiana Territory, on August 11, 1810.

4. William Henry Harrison in a letter to the U.S. War Department, quoted in Benjamin Drake, *Life of Tecumseh and, of his brother, the Prophet (Tenskwautawa): With a Historical Sketch of the Shawanoe Indians* (Cambridge, NJ: Harvard University, 1856), 142.

5. Tecumseh, quoted in Matilda Ridout Edgar and Thomas Ridout, *Ten Years in Upper Canada in Peace and War, 1805–1815: Being the Ridout Letters* (Toronto: W. Briggs), 231.

6. Tecumseh , quoted in Ethel T. Raymond, *The Chronicles of Canada, Volume 17: Tecumseh* (Toronto: Glasgow, Brook and Co., 1920), 136.
7. Tecumseh in Drake, 133.
8. Tecumseh to Proctor, October 1813.
9. Shabonna, quoted in Solon Robinson, *Me-Won-I-Toc* (Cambridge, NJ: Harvard University Press, 1867), 32.

Chapter Six: Red George and the Highlanders

1. Quoted in John J. O'Gorman, "Canada's Greatest Chaplain," *The Catholic Historical Review*, Vol. 8, No. 2 (July 1922), 225.

Chapter Seven: John Strachan and the Defence of York

1. Quoted in William John Karr, *Explorers, Soldiers and Statesmen*: *A History of Canada Through Biography* (Toronto: Ayers Publishing, 1970), 218.
2. A series of letters from Roger Sheaffe to George Prevost, quoted in Lieutenant-Colonel E. Cruickshank, Ed., *A Documentary History of the Campaign upon the Niagara Frontier* (Lundy's Lane Historical Society, 1901), 186–201.
3. A.N. Bethune, *Memoir of the Right Reverend Strachan: First Bishop of Toronto* (Toronto: Henry Roswell, 1870).
4. Dr. John Strachan in a letter to Dr. James Brown, St. Andrews, York, April 26, 1813.
5. Quoted in Charles Humphries, "The Capture of York," Morris Zaslow, Ed., *The Defended Border*, (Toronto: Macmillan Company of Canada, 1964), 258.
6. Dr. John Strachan in a letter to Dr. James Brown, St. Andrews, York, April 26, 1813.
7. Benn, 78.

Chapter Eight: The Voltigeurs

1. Lieutenant Charles Pinguet in a letter to his brother, quoted in Don Gilmour, Pierre Turgeon, *Canada: A People's History* (Toronto: McClelland & Stewart Ltd., 2000), 175.

Chapter Nine: The Sea Wolves

1. Quoted in J. Mackay Hitsman, *Safeguarding Canada, 1763-1871* (Toronto: University of Toronto Press, 1968), 114.
2. Commodore Sir James Yeo to Lord Thomas Melville, May 30, 1815.
3. Cockburn, quoted in Roger Morriss, *Cockburn and the British Navy in Transition: Admiral Sir George Cockburn* (Charlotte: University of South Carolina Press, 1997), 93.
4. "Blockade of the Chesapeake," *Niles Weekly Register*, Saturday, April 23, 1812.
5. Charles Geoffrey Muller, *The Darkest Day: The Washington-Baltimore Campaign of the War of 1812* (Philadelphia: University of Pennsylvania Press, 2003), 59.
6. Lieutenant Gleig, quoted in Muller, 104.
7. Quoted in Dolly Madison, *Memoirs and Letters of Dolly Madison, Wife of James Madison, President of the United States* (New York: Houghton, Mifflin and Company, 1887), 104.
8. Ross's Report of August 30, 1814.

Chapter Ten: The Lords of the Sea

1. *Nova Scotia Royal Gazette*, July 1, 1812.
2. Letter of Marque for the *Liverpool Packet*, Issued by the Vice Admiralty Court on November 19, 1812.
3. Almira Paul, *The Surprising Adventures of Almira Paul* (Boston: N. Coverley, 1816), 4.
4. Paul, 5.
5. Paul, 20.

Chapter Eleven: The Man of the Future

1. William Hamilton Merritt, *Journal of Events, Principally on the Detroit and Niagara Frontiers, During the War of 1812* (Cambridge, MA: Harvard University Historical Society, 1863), 45.

2. Dr. William Dunlop, *Recollections of the American War 1812–1814* (Toronto: Historical Publishing Co., 1905), 55.

SELECT PRIMARY SOURCES

Bethune, A.N. Ed. *Memoir of the Right Reverend Strachan: First Bishop of Toronto.* Toronto: Henry Roswell, 1870.

Dunlop, Dr. William. *Recollections of the American War 1812–1814.* Toronto: Historical Publishing Co., 1905.

Firth, Edith. *The Town of York, 1793–1815: A Collection of Documents of Early Toronto.* Toronto: The Champlain Society, 1962.

Madison, Dolly. *Memoirs and Letters of Dolly Madison, Wife of James Madison, President of the United States.* New York: Houghton, Mifflin and Company, 1887.

Merritt, William Hamilton. *Journal of Events, Principally on the Detroit and Niagara Frontiers During the War of 1812.* Cambridge, NJ: Harvard University Historical Society, 1863.

Paul, Almira. *The Suprising Adventures of Almira Paul.* Boston: N. Coverley, 1816.

Public Archives of Canada. *Report of the Public Archives of Canada.* Ottawa: Public Archives of Canada, 1896.

Ridout, Matilda and Thomas Ridout, Eds. *Ten Years in Upper Canada in Peace and War, 1805–1815: Being the Ridout Letters.* Toronto: W. Briggs, 1885.

Tupper, Ferdinand Brock, Ed. *The Life and Correspondence of Major-General Sir Isaac Brock.* London: Simpkin, Marshall and Co., 1845.

SELECT SECONDARY SOURCES

Allen, Robert. *His Majesties Allies: British Indian Policy in the Defence of Canada, 1774–1775*. Toronto: Dundurn Press, 1996.

Antal, Sandy. *A Wampum Denied: Proctor's War of 1812*. Ottawa: Carleton University, 1997.

Benn, Carl. *Historic Fort York: 1793–1993*. Winnipeg: Natural History/Natural Heritage Inc., 1993.

_____. *The Iroquois in the War of 1812*. Toronto: University of Toronto Press, 1998.

_____. *The War of 1812*. Toronto: Osprey Publishing, 2002.

Campey, Lucille H. *The Scottish Pioneers of Upper Canada From 1784–1855*. Toronto: Natural Heritage/Natural History Inc., 2005.

Chartrand, Rene and Gerry Embleton. *British Forces in North America, 1793–1815*. Toronto: Osprey Publishing, 1998.

Coffin, William Foster. *1812: The War and Its Moral*. Montreal: John Lovell, 1864.

Cruickshank, Lieutenant-Colonel E., Ed. *A Documentary History of the Campaign Upon the Niagara Frontier*. Lundy's Lane: Lundy's Lane Historical Society, 1901.

Drake, Benjamin. *Life of Tecumseh and, of His Brother, the Prophet (Tenskwautiawa): With a Sketch of the Shawanoe Indians*. Cambridge, NJ: Harvard University Press, 1856.

Eckert, Allan W. *A Sorrow in Our Heart: The Life of Tecumseh*. Toronto: Random House, 2000.

FitzGibbon, Mary Agnes. *A Veteran of 1812: The Life of James FitzGibbon*. Toronto: William Briggs, 1894.

Fredrikson, John C. *America's Military Adversaries: From Colonial Times to the Present*. Santa Barbara: ABC-CLIO Inc., 2001.

Gilmore, Don and Pierre Turgeon. *Canada: A People's History*. Toronto: McClelland and Stewart, 2000.

Hickey, Donald R. *The War of 1812: A Forgotten Conflict*. Chicago: University of Illinois, 1989.

James, William. *Naval Occurences of the War of 1812*. New York: Naval Institute Press, 2004.

Johnson, Rossiter. *A History of the War of 1812–1815 Between the United States and Britain*. California: Dodd, Mead and Co., 1882.

Karr, William John. *Explorers, Soldiers and Statesmen: A History of Canada Through Biography*. Toronto: Ayers Publishing, 1970.

Kelton, Dwight H. *Annals of Fort Michilimackinac*. Detroit: Detroit Free Press Publishing, 1882.

Moriss, Roger. *Cockburn and the British Navy in Transition: Admiral Sir George Cockburn*. Charlotte: University of South Carolina Press, 1997.

Muller, Charles Geoffrey. *The Darkest Day: The Washington-Baltimore Campaign of the War of 1812*. Pennsylvania: University of Pennsylvania Press, 2003.

Nelson, Paul David. *General Sir Guy Carleton, Lord Dorchester*. Danvers: Associated University Press, 2000.

Nursey, Walter R. *The Story of Sir Isaac Brock*. Toronto: McClelland and Stewart, 1923.

Nute, Grace Lee. *The Voyageur*. St. Paul: Minnesota Historical Society, 1931.

Ontario Historical Society. *The Defended Border: Upper Canada and the War of 1812*. Toronto: Macmillan Canada, 1864.

Randall, Henry Stevens. *The Life of Thomas Jefferson, Vol. 3*. California: Derby and Johnson, 1858.

Read, David Breakenridge. *The Life and Times of Major-General Sir Isaac Brock, K.B.* California: W. Briggs, 1894.

Robinson, Solon. *Me-Won-I-Toc*. Cambridge, NJ: Harvard University Press, 1867.

Roosevelt, Theodore. *The Naval War of 1812.* New York: G.P. Putnam's Sons, 1900.

Smyth, Sir James Carmichael. *Precis of the Wars in Canada: From 1775 to the Treaty of Ghent in 1814.* New York: C. Rosworth, 1826.

Tucker, Glen. *Tecumseh: Visons of Glory.* New York: Cosimo, 2005.

Wrong, George M. and H.H. Langton, Eds. *The Chronicles of Canada.* Glasgow: Brook and Co., 1920.

Zaslow, Morris, Ed. *The Defended Border.* Toronto: Macmillan of Canada, 1964.

ACKNOWLEDGEMENTS

The author would like the staff at the Archives of Ontario and Library and Archives of Canada for their professionalism, dedication, and assistance in locating images and resources for this book.

INDEX

BY THE SAME AUTHOR

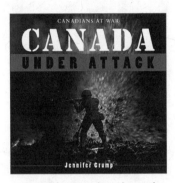

Canada Under Attack
Jennifer Crump
978-1-554887316 / $19.99

Canadians have been celebrated participants in numerous conflicts on foreign soil, but most Canadians aren't aware that they've also had to defend themselves many times at home. From U.S. General Benedict Arnold's covetous attempts to declare Canada the 14th colony during the American Revolution to the German U-boat battles in the Gulf of St. Lawrence in the Second World War, Canada has successfully defended itself against all invaders.

Jennifer Crump brings to life the battles fought by Canadians to ensure the country's independence, from the almost ludicrous Pork n' Beans War to the deadly War of 1812. She reveals the complex American and German plans to invade and conquer Canada, including the nearly 100-page blueprint for invading Canada commissioned by the U.S. government in 1935 — a scheme that remains current today!

MORE GREAT DUNDURN
TITLES FOR YOUNG ADULTS

To Stand and Fight Together
Richard Pierpoint and the Coloured Corps of Upper Canada
Steve Pitt
978-1-550027310 / $19.99

In 1812, a 67-year-old black United Empire Loyalist named Richard Pierpoint helped raise "a corps of Coloured Men to stand and fight together" against the Americans who were threatening to invade the tiny British colony of Upper Canada.

Pierpoint's unique fighting unit would not only see service throughout the War of 1812, it would also be the first colonial military unit reactiviated to quash the Rebellion of 1837. It would go on to serve as a police force, keeping the peace among the competing Irish immigrant gangs during the construction of the Welland Canal.

Pierpoint and the Coloured Corps are the central focus, but the sidebars featuring fascinating facts about the rise and fall of slavery in North America and the state of African-Canadians in early Canada provide an entertaining and informative supplement. Among other tidbits, readers will find out why "Good Queen Bess" launched the British slave industry and how Scottish pineapples are connected to the American Declaration of Independence.

Men of Steel
Canadian Paratroopers in Normandy, 1944
Bernd Horn
978-1-554887088 / $19.99

Take a trip back in time to the chaos and destruction of the greatest invasion in military history, viewed through the lens of Canadian paratroopers. *Men of Steel* is the exciting story of some of Canada's toughest and most daring soldiers in the Second World War.

In the dead of night, on June 5, 1944, hundreds of elite Canadian paratroopers hurled themselves from aircraft behind enemy lines. That daring act set the stage for the eventual success of the Allied invasion fleet. From aircraft formations striking out from England on a turbulent flight across the English Channel to the tumultuous drop over Occupied Europe and deadly close combat in the Normandy countryside, *Men of Steel* is a detailed account of Canadian paratroopers and their instrumental role in D-Day.

Available at your favourite bookseller.

 **DUNDURN PRESS**
www.dundurn.com

What did you think of this book?
Visit www.dundurn.com for reviews, videos, updates, and more!